Patricia Treece

A MAN
FOR OTHERS

Maximilian Kolbe
Saint of Auschwitz
In the Words of Those
Who Knew Him

1817
Published in San Francisco by
HARPER & ROW PUBLISHERS
Cambridge, Hagerstown, New York, Philadelphia
London, Mexico City, São Paulo, Sydney

FIRST EDITION

Designed by Leigh McLellan

Library of Congress Cataloging in Publication Data

Treece, Patricia.
  A MAN FOR OTHERS.

  Bibliography
    1. Kolbe, Maximilian, 1894–1941.   2. Franciscans—
Poland—Biography.   3. Christian martyrs—Poland—
Biography. I. Title.
  BX4705.K625T73   1982   271′.3′024 [B]   82–48404
  ISBN 0–06–067069–X

82 83 84 85 86 10 9 8 7 6 5 4 3 2 1

Contents

To all the unknown saints: gentile and
Jew, Gypsy and German, all races and
faiths—then and now. Thank you for
showing us that sanctity is stronger than
sadism, that compassion can outlast cruelty,
and that—in the face of the greatest evil—
good wins mysterious but real victories for
our human race.

And to another little poor man,
Brother Francis Mary of Marytown, USA,
who made this book possible.

Prologue

Auschwitz, 1941. The sergeant, a tough professional soldier, has just been fingered by an SS man for one of the cruelest deaths here. He is to be shut up naked in an empty, subterranean cell and left without food or water until he dies.

Grown men not too numbed by terror wail and weep at such a sentence. This victim is no exception. He is sobbing over his wife and children, and saying he doesn't want to die.

The SS ignore him.

Suddenly another prisoner, breaking ranks, asks to take the condemned man's place. Even the SS are stunned. Having reduced the personal identities of twenty thousand Poles to numbers, for once they want to know more about a victim.

"Who are you?" one SS man asks number 16,670.

"A Catholic priest," the prisoner replies. "I have no family," he adds, as though that explains everything. An undercurrent runs through the camp: "It's Father Kolbe." Even those who are not his friends recognize the name—the famous Franciscan, the editor, publisher, and opinion-molder whose publications were so influential in prewar Poland.

What is he thinking of? Even the Bible of his faith says only, "Greater love than this has no man—that he lay down his life for a friend." The doomed man is not even a friend of Kolbe's.

"Well, you see," one of Kolbe's intimates interjects, "for Father Kolbe everyone is a friend."

"Now there's a Polish hero for you!" someone exclaims.

"A real saint," murmurs another.

"A fool, you mean," mutters a third.

The sergeant, after the initial shock of relief when Kolbe's offer is accepted, will fall into an almost suicidal depression over Kolbe's having died for him. Then, one day, he suddenly sees himself as a man with a mission: To survive so word of the Franciscan's free-will offering of his life for a fellow human being will survive, too, to enrich the human family.

He does not know that others, even before Kolbe's arrest by the Gestapo, thought that the Franciscan was a never-to-be-forgotten person, a credit to the human race because of the way he gave himself freely and completely to others, whatever their class, race, religion or condition.

"Pray that I will love without any limits," he had written his mother when still in his twenties. That prayer, feel those who know him, has been abundantly answered. They point to Kolbe's turning the Franciscan friary he founded into a hospice for displaced Polish Jews, gentiles, and German invaders alike, with a sense of brotherhood that simply did not include the words "enemy" or "unlovable" in its vocabulary.

Students of mysticism also point to Kolbe's remarkable life and sacrificial death. They speak of it as evidence of the highest spirituality, that of an individual completely at one with the eternal Goodness who feels he has received, gratuitously, so much love from God that he has to pass it on at any cost. For them, Kolbe simply overflowed with a love so affirming, accepting, and self-giving that he is a spring of water for a thirsty world.

Can a human being really achieve such completeness? Has a man perhaps been lost in myth? Or, if the superhero is real, can we still consider him a member of our so-fallible race? Those who can say, "I was a friend of Maximilian Kolbe," insist he was not only a hero and "another St. Francis" but so down to earth, so simple, so fully, joyously human in his laughter and jokes, his heartaches and sufferings, his problems and pains, that he was the most approachable of friends.

"There was something about him that drew one to him like a magnet. I can only say I just loved to be with him, no matter what the situation or what we were doing," his contemporaries say again and again. Let these people, most of whom are still living—his schoolmates, his Franciscan coworkers, his spiritual children, his prison cellmates, jailers, and concentration camp companions— present us with the laughing, loving, suffering, flesh-and-blood man who gave his life totally to God in service to humanity long before he sealed that gift by bearing the burden of another man's death.

1

The Boy

I HAVE ALWAYS KNOWN Father Maximilian was going to die a martyr because of an extraordinary event in his childhood — but I don't recall whether the thing happened before or after his first confession. One time I didn't like something about him, and I said to him, "My little [son], I don't know what's going to become of you!" After this I never thought again about my remark, but I soon noticed that my child changed so much he was unrecognizable. We had a little hidden altar [in the house] at which he was frequently hiding himself. In general his behavior seemed older than his years. He was always recollected, serious, and praying with tears in his eyes. I got worried that perhaps he was ill, so I asked him, "What's wrong with you?" I insisted, "You have to tell Mama everything."

Trembling and with tears in his eyes, he told me, "When you said to me, 'What will become of you?' I prayed very hard to Our Lady to tell me what *would* become of me. And later in the church I prayed again. Then the Virgin Mother appeared to me holding in her hands two crowns, one white and one red. She looked at me with love and she asked me if I would like to have them. The white meant that I would remain pure and the red that I would be a martyr.

"I answered yes, I wanted them. Then the Virgin looked at me tenderly and disappeared.

"Now anytime I go to church with you and Daddy," he told me, "I imagine it isn't you two but Saint Joseph and Our Lady with me."

The extraordinary change in my boy showed the truth of the thing. He was always thinking about it and, whenever there was the opportunity, with a shining face he talked to me of his desire for a martyr's death. . . .

He talked about it only with her, however. It was she who mentioned the boy's experience to various relatives. From his mouth, even his closest friends never heard a word as long as he lived. To most of them, Maria Dabrowska Kolbe's account late in 1941 provided a key to Kolbe's sanctity,* his theological interests, his unique Marian approach to Christ, his choice of a life's work, and his mode of death. Others continued to appreciate Father Maximilian's extraordinary ability to love and his heroism in a concentration camp, while believing that visions—even those of mystics—are exercises in imagination.[1]

Of course he was not known as Father Maximilian—or even as Max—in childhood. Born a subject of Czar Nicholas II in the town of Zdunska Wola on January 8, 1894,† he was baptized Raymond. He was the second of five sons (only three of whom would live) for Julius Kolbe and Maria Dabrowska, who eked out a subsistence living as piecework weavers, a trade that had been in the family for at least two generations.

If the Kolbes were poor, their country was in even worse shape: Poland existed only in history books, its lands having been partitioned among Russia, Austria, and Prussia. In a world of Russian passports, the Russian calendar, schools taught in Russian, and vigorous campaigns to make residents of the acquired territory "think Russian," the Kolbes clung fiercely to their Polish identity. It was a fitting upbringing for one who later would live with ap-

---

* "Not that he is a saint because he had a vision," explains Franciscan Brother Camillus Dulude, "but that one can say he became a saint because of this vision. In other words, he sensed his responsibility to respond to Mary and, from that point on, his life can be seen as his response to Our Lady's designs on him. Studying his life and writings, what impresses me is just this very personal relationship he had the rest of his life with Mary."

† According to the Gregorian calendar used in most of the world. By the czar's Julian calendar, the date was December 27, 1893.

parent ease in two worlds: The world of material reality and the spiritual world of the mystic.

The heart of the Kolbes' Polish identity was their religion. Russians were Orthodox; being Catholic was, to them, synonymous with being Polish. The rallying point of Polish patriotic and religious fervor was the shrine to the Virgin Mary—frequently hailed as Queen of Poland—at Czestochowa, to which the devout Kolbes pilgrimaged many times. Thus from the beginning of his life, Kolbe's deep spirituality had the Pole's typically Marian stamp.

His cousin Francis Langer, who was just a few months older (and who would also be imprisoned in a Nazi concentration camp), recalls:

> My cousin Raymond had the same disposition as his mother—always smiling. And, just like her, he loved to stay and pray in the church. My mother used to say that if you couldn't find her sister, Maria, you always looked for her in just one place—the church. My parents were very close to Julius and Maria and we all visited back and forth a lot until the Kolbes moved away. I remember Raymond as healthy, well-proportioned, and jolly. We never fought when we played. In general, I'd characterize him as an unusually good boy. I know my mother thought he was a model and used to hold him up to us, her own children, as an example.

Anna Kolbe Galert, an aunt on Kolbe's father's side, was less impressed:

> Raymond used to visit my parents rather frequently. At that period he didn't excel in anything; there was nothing remarkable about him. He was easygoing and, like the others, active and quick.

An independent, fun-loving boy, Raymond related openly to God without the slightest embarrassment, as this recollection of a childhood playmate illustrates. Raymond and his friends were headed home late in the day, scuffing their toes along the sidewalks and weary from hard play. It was well past the hour when Raymond was supposed to be back. Afraid of what his mother would do, he begged the others, "Will you do me a favor? Will you say a Hail Mary with me that either my mom won't punish me or else she'll only punish me a little?"

By the time Raymond was six, his family had lived in several cities and villages, trying always to better their lot. Around 1904 and 1905, Maria Kolbe was operating a small store out of the family home in the city of Pabianice,* working with Julius in a factory, and doing business as a midwife. Julius further supplemented their income by renting some small plots and growing vegetables.

The Kolbes didn't have much money—nor did they want much, as Maria later explained, because they felt wealth was an obstacle to spiritual advancement. Their poverty posed a problem when it came time to educate their sons, however. Schooling under the czar was so expensive that many people in the Polish regions remained illiterate. A family that could educate even one child was considered fortunate, and that is all that the hardworking Kolbes felt they could manage. They chose Francis, the eldest. Raymond helped his mother mind the tiny store, care for his younger brothers Joseph and Anthony (who died at age four when Raymond was ten), and do housework. He made no fuss, recalls Maria Dabrowska, and used to please her by inventing new dishes when she was out on a case and he had to cook. She went on to say:

> One day I had a patient who needed a poultice and I sent my little Raymond to the pharmacy to buy the necessary powder. When he asked for some "vincon greca," the pharmacist asked him how he knew it by that name. Raymond answered, "Because that's the way it's called in Latin."
>
> "But how do you know it has a name in Latin?"
>
> "Because we go to the priest's house and learn Latin."
>
> The pharmacist kept asking questions — what was his name, where did he live, and what school did he go to.
>
> Raymond told him that his big brother was attending school and, "if the good Lord permits, he's going to be a priest. But I have to help at home. My parents can't send us both to school. They don't have enough money."
>
> The pharmacist then said, "My boy, to leave you like this is a pity. Come to me. I'll give you lessons. By the end of the year, you'll be caught up with your brother and pass the same exams he does." He set

---

*Population 32,346 in 1900.

the hours for the lessons. After this my dear little Raymond flew to me as if he had wings. With great joy he told me the wonderful thing that had happened to him. And in fact from that day on, he went to the pharmacist for lessons. This good and heaven-sent man — his name was Kotowski — prepared him in such a way that he caught up with his older brother and they passed the examinations together for entering the next year's class.

How they did it Maria Kolbe does not explain, but somehow they managed for one year, 1906, to send both boys to school—a school taught in Polish, a concession gained only the previous year. In 1907 Conventual Franciscans from the Austrian zone came to Pabianice and gave a parish mission. They were scouting for vocations in the czar's territory, where Roman Catholic friaries, monasteries, and convents had been largely ousted after an insurrection in 1873. In Francis and Raymond, they thought they might have prime candidates. At least they had two eager applicants whose parents, themselves third order Franciscans,* believed their sons could aspire to no finer life. In 1907 Raymond was about thirteen, his brother a year older. The Franciscans offered a good deal: feeding, boarding, and educating teenage boys who might or might not eventually decide to take vows as Franciscans.

Disguised as farmers, Julius Kolbe and his sons undertook the clandestine crossover into Austrian territory. The boys completed the rest of their journey by themselves to what the Austrians called Lemberg, the Poles Lwow, and today—as part of Russia—is known as L'vov.

That was the end of family life for Raymond and, shortly thereafter, even for his parents. One accepted progression in Hinduism is for an individual to be a householder for a period and then—at a new stage of development, having fulfilled obligations to society and family—to set that aside and become a full-time spiritual seeker. This progression is not common in Catholic families, but it is by no means unknown. To the deeply religious Kolbes, it seemed the proper course. In a document dated July 9, 1908, Julius Kolbe renounced his marital rights and gave his wife, who had longed to

---

*An association of those living outside friaries but striving—whatever their occupation—for spiritual wholeness (i.e., holiness) according to the spirit of Saint Francis.

be a nun as a girl,* permission to consecrate herself exclusively to the service of God. He pronounced his own readiness to take vows of chastity and went to a Franciscan monastery. His wife and Joseph, the youngest living son (two years younger than Raymond, he was twelve that year) went to Lwow, where Francis and Raymond were studying with the Franciscans. Joseph spent the years 1908 to 1910 in Saint Casimir's boarding school there, then followed his brothers into the Franciscan minor seminary. To be near her three boys Maria stayed with Benedictine nuns in Lwow until 1913, when she moved to Cracow. There she served as a portress with the Felician Sisters, also third order Franciscans, until her death in March 1946.

Julius, who was characterized by a fellow weaver as "a man everybody loved," eventually left the friary—because of a Superior, it is said, who didn't like the intelligent Kolbe's innovative ways. He then opened a religious goods store in Poland's great shrine town, Czestochowa. When World War I broke out, he fought with other Poles for liberation from Russia. According to Father Maximilian, his father simply disappeared, as did thousands of others. There is some evidence that, taken prisoner because he had been technically a subject of the czar, Julius was summarily executed (most likely by hanging) as a traitor.

Some have wondered whether the family broke up because they were unhappy. Family friend John Traczyk, who accompanied the Kolbe family to Pabianice and lived there until 1907, the year the older boys entered the seminary, would have scoffed at the idea. He "used to go to the Kolbe's several times a week" for secret meetings dealing with political and religious liberation from the Russians. Traczyk admired the fact that Julius "wasn't afraid of having these secret meetings in his house." He was also often with the Kolbes, he says, because he and they (undoubtedly with others) "had founded an association to honor the Eucharist." He characterizes them as "a perfect family—outstanding from a patriotic and religious point of view":

> I never saw the parents angry at their children and I never heard them
> complain that their children were disobedient, misbehaved in the neigh-

---

*The Catholic convents had been largely supplanted by those of the Russian Orthodox Church.

borhood, or didn't do well in school. Everybody could see that these good and virtuous parents worked with all their strength to educate their sons. And the boys were good children — easy to handle and obedient. Nobody ever complained about those children. I have very fond memories of those years in which I was so often with the Kolbe family. . . .

---

1. Kolbe has been singled out through canonization by the Catholic Church as a man who loved God and others authentically to the point of heroism. But even canonizing someone does not imply, the church affirms, that any visions the individual may have had are supernatural rather than self-induced. Common sense seconds what Church and psychology maintain: many visions come out of the subconscious or imagination. Some of these are harmless and quickly forgotten; some may have positive results, such as a sense of peace; some are dangerous, because they indicate a break with reality or are part of a problem in relating to others (a support for the feeling of being different or superior, perhaps).

The student of such matters cannot avoid the fact that some visions, like some dreams, seem to tap into a source of negativity so profound that it apparently lies even beyond the personal subconscious. Some visions of this type bear strange fruit: beyond causing the recipient to feel superior to others, they may even lead to an individual proclaiming himself a seer, prophet, or savior and founding a new religion based on the truth revealed "for the first time ever."

Other visions, again like some dreams, seem to tap into a great reservoir beyond the personal unconscious that some call the collective unconscious, some call God. Here at the outer edges are found those rare visions—some would include Kolbe's—that are the impetus for a life of joyous self-fulfillment spent, paradoxically, in humble self-denial and service to others, not as a superior being but as an individual who has received so much love he simply has to pass it on.

2

The Student

WHEN HE ENTERED the Franciscan minor seminary in Lwow, Raymond became good friends with Bronislaus Stryczny, another new boy, who was a year or two older. Many years later, Stryczny narrowly survived imprisonment in Dachau. Later sent by the Franciscans to work in the United States, he died on August 14, 1974, the thirty-third anniversary of Kolbe's death, in Santa Maria, California. From his reminiscences:

> My friend distinguished himself in school by his effort and hard work. We students and especially our teachers marveled at his deep and unusual grasp of mathematics. In no time he used to solve the most difficult mathematical assignments, ones that the rest of us and even the teachers needed much time and paper to conclude! He was more than kind to us and ready to help us with our mathematical difficulties. No wonder he won our goodwill!
>
> Already [between 1907 and 1910] he anticipated the possibility of reaching the moon with a rocket and he thought of many other unusual inventions. . . . As students, he and I took outings in the hills around Lwow. Our conversations most often centered on such matters.

Another classmate, Ladislaus Dubaniowski, left the minor seminary and entered a diocesan one, later becoming a parish priest.

He recalls Raymond Kolbe in the sole year (1908–1909) that they were classmates:

> We talked a lot about Poland's future, discussing among other things how to liberate Lwow. He distinguished himself from the rest of us, I thought, in the exceptional way he carried out his religious practices — the way he said the Rosary or adored the Blessed Sacrament. I recall his kneeling in the first row in the choir as a rule, in order to avoid the distractions caused by his companions.
>
> In difficulties, he didn't get depressed or cave in; on the contrary, he said joyfully, "Next time everything will be all right." This attitude, I'm convinced, did not arise from his psychic disposition (although I believe he had a serene and joyful temperament), but from his profound confidence in the Mother of God.
>
> When he suffered some pain or sadness of soul, he didn't mention it but controlled himself. I would say this was even heroic. I noticed too how, to train himself spiritually, he would sometimes distribute his share to others when we got fruit, which I know he liked very much. He often said that he desired to consecrate his entire life to a great idea, but he did not specify what the idea was.
>
> Among us, he played the role of the fellow that everyone could trust.

Although Dubaniowski apparently never saw Kolbe after leaving the Franciscans' minor seminary, he says, "I pray for his intercession everyday."

It is possible that, precociously spiritual himself, he had unusual insight into the adolescent Kolbe. It is also likely that at the same time he may have, in the way of fifteen-year-olds, somewhat idealized his classmate. At least Stryczny, the lifelong friend, remembers a less perfectly controlled figure. He says:

> I remember a day when we had a quarrel. Because of his last name, I hurled at him the epithet, "You, German!" He burst into tears.

Kolbe was an honor student who excelled in math and the physical sciences, diagrammed model rockets, planned interplanetary flights, and made wireless sets and other scientific apparatus. He was also very interested, according to Dubaniowski and others, in military matters, strategy, and fortifications. He drew up an extensive set of plans for the strategic defense of Lwow that resolved detailed problems. All his life he loved to play chess. In these days, he also liked to use the many sets of pawns he made to work out military maneuvers. Gruchala, a layman who taught him math, remarked ruefully, "What a pity this boy's becoming a priest when he has so many talents!"

Raymond, too, wondered. In September 1910, after three years of junior seminary, he was notified by the Franciscans that he had been accepted into their novitiate. He desired to be consecrated to Mary, but he had become convinced he was in some way to be her soldier for God. Just as St. Francis, who was told in a vision to "Build up my Church," began gathering bricks to repair San Damiano before he understood the larger implications of the message, Kolbe prepared to leave the Franciscans and enlist in the military. In his excitement over using his talents as a military inventor and strategist, Raymond also convinced his older brother Francis (whether he intended to or not) to leave the Franciscans. They were actually on their way to inform the Prior when their mother appeared for one of her frequent visits. No one knows what Maria Dabrowska Kolbe said—but the boys reversed their decision. Raymond became a novice and was given the name Maximilian. Apparently he never had a regret, for nine years later he wrote:

> How can I forget the moment when Francis and I, waiting for our appointment with Father Provincial to tell him we did not wish to enter the Order, heard the bell ring in the reception room. At that very delicate moment the God of providence, in his infinite mercy and through the services of Mary Immaculate, sent me my mother.

Of their time in the novitiate, Stryczny reports:

> After the novitiate began, we talked on our outings into the hills more along religious themes. It was at that time we established a lifelong friendship and promised to recite for each other a daily "Hail Mary." We decided that, after receiving ordination to the priesthood, we would remember one another at Mass to the end of our lives. After the death of one of us, the other was to keep this promise until we met again in heaven. Our conversations were often on the ways to further develop our spiritual life.

During the 1910–1911 school year, Father Bronislaus, older and more experienced, was given charge of his roommate Max (as he was now called) by their Superiors during the latter's sudden se-

vere attack of scruples. In such cases the sufferer is tortured by
thoughts of letting God down, broods over the possible culpability
of his most innocent or unthinking acts, and inflates his real sins—
however paltry—out of all proportion. The time-honored cure for
scruples is complete openness to another person and absolute obedience to his advice. Max was told to confide each anxiety—no
matter how silly or intimate it sounded aloud—*immediately* to
Bronislaus, whose counsel on the matter was to be strictly followed. The remedy was completely successful. As an aftereffect of
the struggle, for the rest of his life Max had special insight into the
problem and a deep empathy for its victims, a combination that
often led to their cure.

On September 5, 1911—four months short of his eighteenth
birthday—Max and others took temporary vows as Friars of the
Conventual Franciscans. The next year he and Bronislaus spent
finishing secondary school.

Orders and dioceses select a few of their most gifted members to
study in Rome. In October 1912, Kolbe was given this honor. In
his first three years at the Pontifical Gregorian University, he concentrated on science and math, including trigonometry, physics,
and chemistry, then settled into doctoral studies for two Ph.D.s—
one there and the other at the Franciscans' International College,
also known as the Collegio.

What was Max like in the seven years he spent in Rome? Gifted, say professors, a great asker of questions, not to annoy, but
because his mind longed to stretch itself, to know. One of his teachers, Father Dominic Stella, recalled:

> His questions were unusual and unexpected, but at the same time
> profound to the point that our rector [Father Bondini], a professor of
> law, remained embarrassed. The rector used to tell me, "Max asks ques-
> tions that I have no idea how to answer."

Another professor, Father Leon Cicchito, laughingly called him
"a real bore—the kind who, as you walk along, plies you endlessly
with questions." Then, becoming serious, Cicchito said, "He was
the most gifted youth I had contact with during that period. He
had a rare natural genius."

His fellow students do not dwell on his intellect, indicating he
wore it lightly and never acquired the labels "slave to his books" or

"pious drudge." To his friends he remained the lively, zest-filled, good companion, willing to help others with their studies (he was noted for his clear explanations). In spite of his good grades, he was very much a "kid," naive and unsophisticated. His interest in inventions continued. Cyril Kita, one of the students from the United States, recalls Kolbe talking about the possibility of an invention that would pick up sound waves from the past so that the voice of Christ could be heard. Andreas Eccher took one of Kolbe's projects, a minutely detailed analysis for a high velocity vehicle to take photographs in outer space, to a Gregorian professor, who found it scientifically correct but prohibitively expensive.

Physically, Kolbe was of medium height, rather slight, very good-looking, but with the cherubic face of a young choir boy even after he had earned his first doctorate (in philosophy) at twenty-one. Both Kita and Eccher rue the way he assumed a sober face, unlike his habitual smiling expression, when confronted with a camera.

Quiricus Pignalberi, who studied with him for two years, admits, "I never thought he would accomplish anything great. He himself certainly never talked that way." Similarly a ninety-one-year-old Franciscan living in the United States, whose Mass Max used to serve, remembers only "a nice kid."

A few in the student body thought they saw more. A close friend of Kolbe's, Franciscan priest Joseph Peter Pal, who died in his native Rumania in 1947 esteemed as a saint, wrote:

> In 1913 I heard from some fellow students that we had a saint among us. I asked an Italian friar to point him out. From then until 1919 when we parted, I saw more than words to persuade me.
>
> Max's brotherly love was really like that in the gospels. When our conversation turned to how little our Franciscan College rules were observed, he made me pray for the transgressors. I never heard him talk badly of anyone. But he suffered to see others disregard the rules . . . he observed so carefully.
>
> His love for the Eucharist and for Mary touched his enormous heart to its deepest fibers. Before or after each school hour, he visited Jesus in the tabernacle. Since both of us were a little sick, we used to take walks with the rector's permission. . . . These were to visit various churches where the Eucharist was exposed for adoration—especially the Sacred

Heart Church near Quirnal Hill, where some French sisters had perpetual adoration. He enrolled as a watcher there.

When he was ordained and began celebrating mass, you could read in his face his immense and total participation.*

His devotion to Our Lady was childlike and sincere. During our walks to the churches and on our return, he made me say the Rosary with him and other Marian prayers such as the Memorare. . . . He used to address Mary sweetly as "Mamma mia."

Once when we were coming back to the Collegio, we met three or four rowdies on their way home from work. They were cursing Our Lady. With tears in his eyes, Max left me in the middle of the road and rushed over to ask why. In confusion, they answered they were just letting off steam. I called to him to leave them alone. But he persisted until he defeated their rage. Never in my life have I met a living person who loved the Madonna more than Max.

Whether he was a saint or not, certainly a tremendous burst of spiritual growth had followed the rocky year of the novitiate. World War I, in which both Julius and Francis† Kolbe were fighting, was a constant topic at the Collegio, which had students from so many countries. Yet Kita recalls that Kolbe "seemed uninterested, and avoided the subject; instead, he talked about spiritual things." Since he must have been intensely interested in at least Poland's struggle to throw off foreign domination, it seems more likely that he was struggling for detachment from his military bent, like the Hindu or Buddhist who leaves loved surroundings for the forest, there to become so totally centered, so enlightened, that he can come back because now it does not matter where he is.

Kolbe's letters and remarks by observers show him growing in

---

* Not everyone did, however. Eccher remarks that Kolbe, from his first Mass on, celebrated devoutly but very normally, with nothing strange or unusual to set him apart.

† Francis applied for a leave of absence to join the military, apparently intending to rejoin the Franciscans after the war. Whether he tried and was refused, as has been claimed, or changed his mind, he was never again in the Order, and later married. John Dagis, a Brother working with Max in the 1920s, recalls that they saw a lot of Francis, Max having gotten him the job of organist when Francis had financial problems. When the Germans invaded in 1939, Francis was again with the military, and was apparently doing intelligence work when he was captured. He was last seen alive on a transport bound for a concentration camp.

that love of God which causes the Christian to reach out to all mankind, longing for others, too, to know and love so good a Father. His naive approach, however, was far from the tact and patience that would later mark his dealings with nonbelievers. Pal recalls how Kolbe wanted the two of them to go at once to convert the head of the Masons, who were staging mass anti-Catholic demonstrations outside St. Peter's. In his enthusiasm, he also bearded people in public conveyances or on the streets. Pal recalled a theological dispute where Kolbe's annoyed adversary snapped, "Listen, young man, don't dispute what I say. I'm a doctor of philosophy," only to have his baby-faced opponent respond, "So am I."

In spite of this youthful urge to deeds, he was starting to surrender himself more and more, in his words, "as a tool in the hands of Mary as she labors to bring all souls to Christ." Those with a Jungian bent will say that, in his Marian devotion, he accepted and integrated his anima (i.e., the healthy feminine components of the male personality), thereby avoiding the severity or coldness of religion that is only in touch with the masculine elements of wholeness.

He wanted to love, as he later put it, "without limits." In this pursuit, he became increasingly enamored of his Franciscan vow of obedience. In writings, letters, and conversations for the rest of his life, he returned to this idea. He wished to act, but only if his superiors approved—for there alone, he felt, was his guarantee that he was not being duped as to God's will. Obedience "alone is the certain criterion of the will of God and consequently of the Immaculata," who became the Mother of God by her fiat ("Let it be done unto me according to Thy Will") and whose will, by her free choice—unlike even angels who fell—remains forever united to God's. Only by relying on obedience, which is not dependent on the goodness or wisdom of the one obeyed but on God's power to act through any instrument, can we "become as unshakable as God." His friend Quiricus Pignalberi recalls that, if the well-liked Kolbe had any peculiarity, it was his unusual attention to the rules of the Order, the Collegio, and the rector. Another classmate, Friar Alberto Arzili, says:

> One day, intending only to tease, I caused him considerable pain.

Having obtained the necessary permission, I took him for a walk to . . . one of Rome's churches. On the way, he asked if I had obtained permission. At my seeming to have neglected that, he became disheartened and so intensely hurt that I quickly confessed in order to reassure him. Then he shook his handsome head with his characteristic gesture and smiled that innocent smile of his which was so appealing.

It is easy to smile at the Kolbe of this period as a cartoon Franciscan or Don Quixote in habit, sweet and sincere but essentially out of touch with reality and hence impotent. This would be a mistake. Although Max was naive, at the same time he was farsighted, not just in scientific areas but in social matters. He saw grave dangers to his Order, his church, and mankind. There were the political dangers of rampant nationalism and Communism, the social dangers of continuing industrialization, materialism, and the rise of the mass media and consequent mass mind, beginning with radio and films. Finally, there were internal dangers in his Order, which needed spiritual renewal.

Rarer still, he was not a condemner but was open to the positive potential in everything. That, too, became a theme: study everything from Communism to show business and see what in it is good; then build on that. When his confreres decried the immorality of films, Max shocked them by saying, "Then let Christians use film to conquer immorality." In the next two decades, while some important Catholic writers continued to rage against technology and heartless industrialism, he would be using machines and techniques borrowed from industry, to the consternation of many who thought "Catholic" synonymous with "medieval."

In the midst of his spiritual and intellectual studies, Max contracted tuberculosis. As he later recalled, one sunny summer day as he was playing soccer, "All of a sudden I felt something come up into my mouth. It was blood." Ordered to bed by the doctor, he says himself, "It seemed that it might be the end." It was not, but he would suffer on and off from serious recurrences the rest of his life.

Gradually, he had learned he was to fight for God under Mary's leadership, not in literal but in spiritual combat. For whatever reason, it was precisely at this low point physically, with his rector's permission, that Max began recruiting members for a spiritual Militia. "The seven saintly founders," he would jokingly call the first group, which was composed mostly of his closer friends. One of these was Pal, who reports:

> The evening of October 16, 1917, we met together in the room next to Father Rector's and Max read to us from a little piece of paper the program outlined by him alone.* . . . I was the first to sign it as I was [already ordained a] priest and the oldest. It seems to me Max signed last. I do not know if this sheet is kept. . . . It would be very interesting, for it shows how Max paid no attention to external appearances, since he used an eighth of a piece of paper to launch such a great work. . . .

The "great work," called the Militia Immaculatae (the Army of Mary Immaculate), did not exactly get off to a rousing start. For a year, in fact, little happened except that two of the seven members died in the 1918 flu epidemic while Max himself, having briefly improved, began hemorrhaging again and had to be suspended from studies for about a month in October. Somehow he managed to handle this life-threatening illness in such a way that some classmates later remarked that they never realized he was ill—he even recruited a few more members. He also took, says Pal, to signing "M.I." after his name, signifying Miles Immaculatae (Soldier of Mary Immaculate). That was about it. Still, his friend Arzili claims to have had no doubts the new organization would eventually amount to something, because Max, he says:

> . . . refused to be blocked by obstacles; the most arduous difficulties seemed to him nothing. . . . His passion, his torment, was for three main things: the union of the Churches, the purity of the peoples' way of life, and the sharing of all persons in the holiness of God. For these goals, his energies flowed.

On July 22, 1919, he received his second doctorate, this one in theology. He was twenty-five. The next day, traveling with Cyril Kita, who was going for a visit before returning to the United States, he left for Poland. Ascetic Father Stephen Ignudi, that

---

* Pal stresses Kolbe's authorship because, in the account of the Militia's founding written by Kolbe himself, the latter manages to imply that many aspects were a group initiative when they were, in fact, his own.

year's rector of the Collegio, noted degree and departure in the college log, then summed up in three words his opinion of Kolbe. The logbook reads:

> Maximilian Kolbe, province of Galicia; arrived Oct. 29, 1912; ordained to the priesthood, April 28, 1918; degree in philosophy from Pontifical Gregorian University; degree in sacred theology from this College, July 22, 1919; departed July 23, 1919. A young saint.

3

At Work

FATHER MAXIMILIAN, as he would be known from now on (except among his old seminary classmates), returned in July 1919 to a homeland the treaties ending World War I had pieced together as a political as well as cultural reality for the first time since the partitions of 1772–1795. That—and little else in Poland—was cause for rejoicing. Devastated by war, the new nation was deathly sick economically, with concomitant political and social ills. The many Jews—one-tenth of the population—whose ancestors had moved to Poland because the country was a haven began to feel the rise of the same anti-Semitism that was festering in war-ruined Germany.

Where a nation and people faced such struggles to stay alive, every hand was useful. In spite of his tuberculosis (which his superiors may have underestimated, since he never mentioned it), Kolbe was appointed professor of theology at the Cracow Franciscan Seminary where he had once been a student. He was not a successful teacher; because of his lung disease, he was unable to speak loudly enough to be effective. Reassigned to hear confessions and preach, he had similar problems. Yet in October, in spite of his precarious health, he received the local bishop's and his Franciscan

Province-level Superior's approval of the Militia. In his free time, he began to recruit members, first among his Order, then among the laity, including students from the University of Cracow (where he also managed to convert the math professor). The time was ripe, for with chaos in the country, people were seeking clear goals, meaning, camaraderie, and an inspiring cause. That of the Militia was simple: to bring the whole world to God through Christ under the generalship of Mary.

Kolbe had things moving well when he collapsed with severe hemorrhages and was sent to the hospital. In August 1920, he was transferred to a tuberculosis sanatorium in the mountain city of Zakopane. In May 1921, he was moved to a convent in Nieszawa, where he remained until November.

While a patient, he had orders from his Superior to drop work for the Militia, and he obeyed. However, he acted as chaplain to the sanatorium where he was a patient and also frequently visited another Zakopane sanatorium, one exclusively for university students. Under the influence of Communism (which was taking hold in neighboring Russia) and other philosophical and social movements, most of the students, he found, were lapsed Catholics, many atheists. Using what for the once so naive Kolbe was a new and infinitely more subtle approach to acquainting people with God, he loaned books, chatted, and offered the bored young people free-wheeling lectures "very informally, so that everyone would express his opinions," as he wrote in a letter to Jerome Biasi, one of the M.I. founders.

The spectacular ability to influence others and draw them to the spiritual life that would be so striking in Kolbe for the rest of his life appeared in evidence for the first time, not when he was in a period of health and success, but—as is so often the case with mystics and saints—just when he seemed useless, his plans for a great work frozen, his health broken. He made so many converts at that sanatorium that the director tried to bar him from the premises. Without a trace of hostility, the young priest replied, "I'll continue to visit here just like anyone else," and he did.

He wrote close friends like Biasi and his mother details of some of his conversions, including one of the director of an atheistic institution in Zakopane that did not allow priests on the premises. Accepting that restriction as a challenge, Kolbe used a ruse—he claimed to need a certain book that could be found only in their library—to get his foot past the obdurate doorman and then proceeded to charm the director so much that he was repeatedly urged to come again. He does not mention his charm, of course. Neither does he mention the things Anna Wojtaniowa Gibas, a Catholic nurse at the student sanatorium, recalls. Because the hospital director, an atheist, had no concern for the students' spiritual lives, Anna took it on herself to call Kolbe to the dying or desperately ill to console them or give the sacraments to believers. She says:

> Very sick, and hospitalized elsewhere himself, he was a true Samaritan. Whenever I called him, he always came right away. . . . Many times this was in the depths of the night or during snowstorms, and he himself might have a fever. In the case of the dying, I noticed he frequently came running without having taken the time to dress adequately against the cold. I remember one night there was a violent rainstorm when I telephoned that there was no time to lose. He came with communion for a dying girl, not at all concerned about the rain or the mud, and left happy.
>
> When he came to lead discussions . . . he conducted these in such a spontaneous and pleasant way that all the sick, even those who had long ago abandoned any religion, loved him.

Back in Cracow before Christmas of 1921, he again began forming units of the Militia, who were organized in homogeneous groups—one for high school students, another for local intellectuals, a third for the Franciscans who had been his first recruits in 1919, and so on. To provide a means of reaching more potential members and keeping in touch with the entire army as it spread, he asked his Superior if he could begin a magazine. He got permission, with the understanding that he was not to expect any financial support from the hard-pressed order or run up any bills they might be liable for.

Apparently there was less than total enthusiasm on the part of some Superiors and colleagues. For instance, Alphonse Orlini, the Minister General of the Franciscans from 1924–1930, later wrote that in the early days the Provincial Superior, Father Pellegrine Haczela, was "completely against Kolbe's works" and was "perplexed for a long time by his innovations" in the Order. For one thing, Franciscans in the Poland of 1922 did not see their apostolic

works as including journalism and, for another, Kolbe was seriously ill. Critics mumbled the old Polish proverb about people who try
to hit the moon with a shoe. Brother Lawrence Podwapinski says
that he was told by an eyewitness, Brother Gabriel Sieminski, who
met Kolbe in Cracow in 1920, that when Kolbe returned from
Rome, a few of his Cracow confreres nicknamed him "Max the
Naive" or "Marmalade" (slow-moving and sticky sweet). Brother
Lawrence himself, in a later period, recalls visiting friaries where
some priests and Brothers ridiculed Kolbe for his strange ideas. "I
myself suffered a lot over this," the Brother adds. If Kolbe had
such critics, it is certain they were reasonable people who could no
more help making fun of this dreamer than twelfth-century Assisi
could help clucking over Bernardone's crazy boy Francis, or her
contemporaries keep from scolding that sixteenth-century "fanatic,
mad dreamer, and extremist" St. Teresa of Avila.

In Poland, where runaway inflation was causing hardship and
ruin, Kolbe many times begged publishing funds from people almost as penniless as himself. A nucleus of Franciscan supporters,
including his blood brother Father Alphonse (Joseph) Kolbe, lent
a hand with the work and wrote twelve of the first sixteen-page
issue's articles, leaving Kolbe himself only four pages to fill. Called
The Knight of the Immaculata or, for short, *The Knight*, the magazine was given away for the most part, its founder distributing it
on street corners. After a few issues the day came when Kolbe had
no money to pay the latest printing bill. His Collegio friend, Quiricus Pignalberi, remembers that years later Max confided in him
what happened:

> Praying hard for Mary's intercession in the church, he looked up and
> saw a sack on the altar. On it was pinned a note: "For my dear mother,
> Mary Immaculate." Inside was money — the exact amount of the bill. He
> took it joyfully to his Superior, who permitted him to use the money.

Shortly thereafter a visiting American priest, Lawrence Cy-
man—to whom the idea of reaching people through the mass media seemed less strange than it did to many Polish Franciscans—
gave Father Maximilian a hundred dollars. With this gift, a press
was purchased, a model so ancient that it bloodied the hands and
tortured the backs of Max and his friends as they handcranked it
about six times for each of the 5,000 copies that was a standard

run. This brutal but money-saving machine apparently was purchased just after his Superior transferred him (to help his health and give his apostolate more space), with two Brother helpers, to a friary at Grodno that had been recently recovered from the ousted Russians. In October 1922, there were four priests and five or six Brothers in residence, but a few rooms could be put at their disposal. Father Orlini, on a visitation from Rome as head of the entire Conventual Franciscan Order, recalls Kolbe and his by then two-press operation at Grodno, where the press run was up to 12,000 and finally, in 1927, to 60,000:

> The friary was small, far outside the city, and the place very poor — simplicity itself. I saw the workroom where the publishing was done — it too was very simple.
>
> My first impression of Kolbe was that he was ingenuous or naive, but I soon realized this was merely an exceptional simplicity and [came to] deeply appreciate his knowledge in even practical matters as I witnessed myself.
>
> At this time he was very thin. His look was very deep — profound, really. In his eyes there was something I can only call celestial. His mannerisms were very modest, and he was a man of few words; but those few were very exact and to the point.
>
> He was liked by everybody.

Brother Lawrence Podwapinski relates that Kolbe and Brother Zeno Zebrowski, a red-haired, nearly illiterate jack-of-all-trades who would one day be revered in Japan as the father of the poor, kept down expenses by sharing not only a coat but a pair of shoes. The one going out wore them, the one at home did without.

Young John Dagis wanted, he says, "to give my life to a cause." Learning printing at a school run by the Salesian Order, he first planned on membership in this group. But in 1926 he changed his mind and went to Grodno to join Kolbe, who had once visited his school. He would stay with him until 1936, when Kolbe was sent to a new post while Dagis was left at the last one. Released from his vows after fourteen years to fight Hitler in Poland's army in exile, Dagis came to the United States after the war, where he now lives near Chicago. This fervent supporter of the Franciscans, who laughingly calls Kolbe "my boss," says he often senses his mentor's presence today and feels Kolbe still guides him in the many dreams in which he appears. Dagis speaks of Kolbe and the early years of the press apostolate:

> When I arrived as a nineteen-year-old at Grodno, Father Maximilian was away, but his brother Alphonse Kolbe [himself arrived at Grodno that same year] received me very nicely, inquired if I needed anything and so forth. I liked Father Alphonse very much. He was a little nervous, which showed in spite of his control, but so good. He taught me photography and how to run an office. I think he understood me even more than Father Maximilian. After a couple weeks, here comes Father Maximilian. They looked very alike. He, too, accepted me very nicely. But before long I began to wonder why I had come to the Franciscans when for so long I had planned to become a Salesian of Don Bosco. Maybe this isn't my vocation, I said to myself. Maybe I'm only here by an accident. I went to Father Maximilian with my problem. He made no attempt to talk me into staying.
>
> "Let me take you to a saintly priest," he said, "and you can talk it over with him." So he took me to a paralyzed Redemptorist in Warsaw, a man from a noble family and author of a life of St. Alphonse Liguori. Father Maximilian left us together and I discussed my quandary with this priest.
>
> When I returned to Grodno, Father Maximilian didn't ask me about my talk. He left me totally unpressured. Then Father Alphonse, who liked me very much, gave me a very nice image that said on it, "You haven't chosen me; I've chosen you," from the Scripture. I thought it over and decided God was calling me to the Franciscans. So I went to Father Maximilian and told him everything was okay.
>
> Father Alphonse used to worry about the financial risks he thought Father Maximilian took in something like buying a new press for the apostolate, relying on God to pay the bill.* He'd say to me, "Lots of times I don't agree with Father Maximilian — sometimes, in fact, I think what he's doing is absolutely ridiculous. But everything always works out all right."

Sometime after the move to Grodno, Kolbe began printing pictures of the Brothers working the press. Imagine a country where

---

*These remarks should be balanced by businessman Eugene Srzednicki's testimony that Kolbe was always careful about paying his bills on time so as not to cause hardship to anyone.

the mental picture of a member of a religious order was a kneeling figure, eyes raised to heaven, hands joined in prayer, and you have some idea of the sensation this caused. Not because they were working—it was known Brothers left off praying to sweep and cook just like Sisters nursed or taught, but the idea of Brothers juxtaposed with twentieth-century technology jolted the villages of Poland, which was still over 60 percent agricultural. It looked modern—even glamorous. Accompanying such daring pictures (a few might have found them disrespectful to religion), in each issue there were always ads, "Become a Knight," and testimonies of happy friars. This too was an innovation. Young men began showing up at the Grodno gates. However, they came not simply to become Franciscans, but insisting they wanted to join Father Kolbe's communications apostolate. Dagis says:

> They flocked into Grodno because it was something new in Poland—this press apostolate. We had soldiers, seminarians, teachers, and young fellows like me—all kinds of people. Many came seeking some kind of glamour and found instead a life calling for lots of sacrifice. Those left quickly.

Brother Bartholomew (Bart) Kalucki, now stationed with the Franciscans in Milwaukee, recalls:

> I saw one of those ads. We didn't get the paper, but someone in my village did, and it was passed around after they finished with it. I was only fifteen when I wrote about coming. I got a nice letter back telling me to wait. They thought I was too young to know what I was doing.

Eventually accepted a year later, he loved learning to set type, first by hand and then by machine.

Although Father Orlini would quote Kolbe as saying, "I am by nature Franciscan," others in the Order watched these new recruits joining not it, but Kolbe, and believed he would eventually break away and start a new Order of his own. Dagis recalls:

> Father Maximilian said, "They suspect we want to break off from the Conventuals and form a new Order. The truth is we want to make the Conventuals such a big Order that all the Franciscans* in the world will want to unite with it.

---

*There are three Franciscan men's Orders: the black-clad Conventuals, or Friars Minor Conventual, as they are formally titled; the Friars Minor Capuchin,

Father Maximilian said anyone who came to join us should stop smoking. It offended his idea of Franciscan poverty. One teacher who had been a heavy smoker stayed, but he had to keep a pencil in his mouth all the time to make it.

During this period when we were at Grodno, things were very hard on Father. His Superior there pressed him to give services to the parish the friary was in charge of. Between these duties and those of his own press apostolate, he was very overworked.

Eventually, Kolbe simply collapsed. He had been ill again in 1922; in 1926 he was rehospitalized with serious tuberculosis for about half the year.

According to Dagis, there was a lot of friction at the monastery over the idea of having a press apostolate there. Others have testified that when the magazine—which was still given away free to anyone who couldn't afford a subscription "even by depriving himself a little" (in Kolbe's words)—began to bring in money from enthusiastic readers, the Grodno Superior wanted to use at least some of this to repair the broken-down friary. Kolbe's Brothers (Albert Olszakowski, Gabriel Sieminski, and Zeno Zebrowski were in this earliest group) and Father Alphonse strenuously objected that the money should not go anywhere but back into the press apostolate. Kolbe tried to act as peacemaker. Eventually a compromise, which Dagis describes, was worked out:

> Father Maximilian was paying room and board in 1926 and 1927 to the friary for each of us. They were doing well off the deal. Still, some of the friars not working in the press apostolate didn't want him there because, for one thing, he was a consumptive, although the doctor said he wasn't dangerous.
>
> The only one among all of them who understood Father Maximilian was Father Fordon. When Father Maximilian got depressed over anything, it was Father Fordon who would encourage him and cheer him up.
>
> Father Maximilian always tried to keep it to himself if he was feeling bad so as not to discourage the rest of us. He always hid things like his sufferings from his poor health. Because he had only one lung* he had

---

brown-robed, bearded Franciscans recognizable by the pointed hoods usually worn back on their shoulders; and the Friars Minor, who also wear brown, the largest order of the three and the second most numerous religious Order in the Church.

*The September 22, 1926, report from the Institute of X-Ray and Physiotherapy in Zakopane shows serious tuberculosis, but it does not mention removal of a lung.

difficulty breathing and this caused him to have tremendous headaches almost constantly, but you never heard it from him. He never complained. On the other hand, if one of us got sick, he would stay with him twenty-four hours if necessary to see he got every possible attention. He neglected himself, never anyone else.

He always treated us Brothers, not as inferior to him, the priest, but as if we were truly his brothers. Later he began to say, "You are my children, I am your father." He shared every hardship with us. In fact, whatever was hard, he was the first one to tackle it, the one who wanted to take the burden, the suffering, upon himself. He tried not to give orders. He wanted rather to convince. But he believed very much in the discipline of obedience — for himself as well as for others. Everyone had his assignment. When you got yours, he left you alone to do it. From time to time the whole group was assembled to give suggestions and ideas. But once something was agreed upon, he expected it would be done that way.

Father Maximilian was completely honest. He never tried to keep up any image of himself or other priests by hiding the truth. For instance, he told us why the leader of our nation, Pilsudski, nominally a Catholic, was very cold to the Church, never received communion, and so forth. Pilsudski confided to a close friend who in his later years had become a priest that when Pilsudski's mother lay dying and called for the last sacraments, he — a known Socialist, which in those days meant someone inimical to the church — went to fetch a priest. The priest responded, "I can't go with you; your family isn't practicing the faith." "But my mother is dying and she wants a priest," Pilsudski protested. The priest still flatly refused. Unable to fulfill his mother's last request, Pilsudski said to his friend, "I literally tore out my hair by handfuls, I was in such torment and rage, and that's why I have no respect for you priests or the Church." Father Maximilian told us this, which cast such shame on the priesthood, very openly.

He was a born astronomer. I remember one night when it was cloudless, he named for us every star and planet visible in our part of the world. He showed us the Milky Way and explained the system of galaxies and other things. His explanations were intensely interesting. He had all the classic books in the field, including Kepler's writings in three volumes. He valued these books.

But when I found one of his Ph.D. diplomas and said, "Why don't we frame this and hang it on the wall?" he took it from me and said, "This isn't anything." Later he told me too many priests thought they were important because of their knowledge.

In his case it was not just knowledge. You can't imagine how rich his imagination was! He didn't just read about things like the celestial bodies — he swallowed it. And he was always dreaming up things, like the time he said all facts must remain as images somewhere and perhaps someday someone would invent something to make the past visible so we could see Jesus' real face.

He was very, very human — that's why he suffered so much. He felt so deeply for everyone. For those who were guilty of something, he wished [not to condemn] but to straighten them out.

I know he understood my obsession with Russia where I had been born to Polish-Lithuanian parents and where my only living relative, my older brother, remained. Rescued by a priest Pope Benedict XV sent in to save children during the famine years 1921–1922 of the Reds–Whites armed struggles, I had breached the sealed Polish–Russian border twice only to be caught, jailed, and expelled each time before I could get to my brother. Father Maximilian himself was learning Russian, thinking the time would come when he would start a mission in Russia.

Others mention that Kolbe always kept up to date on all the sociological publications and atheistic literature of the Communists, believing that it was by knowing well and seeing what was good in Communism that Christians could best get across their own message. A very few years later, a Communist visiting Kolbe and his workers in their friary would exclaim, "This is the real Communism right here, the way you're living!" Dagis continues:

Because it's the practice in all friaries, we had many hours of silence, but during our recreation periods each day, Father Maximilian was very good-humored. He loved to tell us little jokes, usually in the form of anecdotes. All these jokes of his were innocent and merry. I remember the one he told us about the town in Italy with three tailors all on one street. The first advertised, "Best tailor in this town." So the second put up a sign, "Best tailor in the world." The third made a small plaque, "Best tailor on this street."

Another time he told us about the absent-minded professor who was reading when the servant brought him a fish for lunch. The professor became hungry after awhile and closed the book, marking his place with the fish. Then he called to the servant, "Where's my lunch?" "I'm afraid it's reading your book" was the reply.

He always laughed with us. ["Oh yes, I've seen him laugh until the tears came to his eyes," confirms Brother Gabriel Sieminski, who first met Kolbe in Cracow in 1920, joined him at Grodno in 1923, and worked with him the rest of Kolbe's life.] But I never saw him either out of control with laughter or seething with temper. In fact, in my ten years close to him, I never saw him angry — and a good part of that time I was working as his secretary. His nerves were very good. His voice always stayed low. He was always calm and good-natured. Above all, he was completely natural. I was even surprised after his death when they began gathering material toward his beatification because his behavior never smacked of the supernatural — at least on the surface. Such simplicity he had! In spite of his extraordinary life, to always behave with such utter naturalness! Rather than show how much he knew or how spiritual he was, he wanted always to be seen as just like those who had less, so everyone would feel his equal. Still, he told us, "You should become great saints," and whatever he asked from somebody, he would have done himself.

Laywoman Sophia Roszkowska says of Kolbe's work in the parish:

For two years, starting in 1922, he came twice a week to the village of Lososna two miles from Grodno to teach religion in the school where I was a teacher. Once a colleague and I also visited him in Grodno, and he showed us their publications, whose progress he was very happy about.

In greeting one he used to offer his hand, saying, "May the Virgin Mary come to your aid!" In leaving, he used the same words. When he crossed the school threshold, it seemed that a being not of this world entered. Sanctity radiated from him so that people fixed their eyes on him, teachers and children alike fascinated. The children longed for his coming and would greet him with applause.

Having taught religion myself, I'm familiar with its problems. Moreover, I've observed the catechetical work of many priests. Thus, from my own experience in the field as well as from wide observation, I can say his catechetical work was extraordinary. The children grasped what religion is all about. They became better and more devout people. Because of his influence, kids were completely changed. It became hard for me to speak of faults or small lies committed by those children. Out of this group came many vocations to religious life.

For them he organized spiritual retreats and he asked us to set up a small shrine to the Immaculata in each class, which he taught the children to adorn with flowers. He also distributed his children's magazine, *The Little Knight,* which they read eagerly.* He founded a school chapter of the M.I., which all the students and teachers joined, and he himself presided over its monthly meetings. During these he asked about the problems of our religious lives or those of our acquaintances. Once I told him about two colleagues, indifferent to religion, who wanted to use a religious shrine as a shooting target until I stopped them. He brought me two Marian medals and asked me to get them to my colleagues.

"The Immaculata will find a way to convert these individuals," he told me, adding, "I feel at peace about them." Once I got over the many difficulties in getting them to accept the medals, they were both converted.

I recall Father Kolbe also used to assist a retired teacher who had no pension with her expenses.

I've seen young people go in groups to the masses celebrated by the Franciscans outside of Grodno, even though this was much further than their own parish church. I knew many of these local young people and I asked them why they went to the friary. They told me they loved to go because of Father Maximilian's mass and his sermons. Adults, too, who had churches close at hand, used to go out to the Franciscans, and they gave me the same reason.

During the time of Kolbe's childhood and young manhood, women were generally held to be inferior. Finland was the only European country in which women could vote—and Kolbe was twelve before that right was granted in 1906. Yet there is not even a hint in the testimonies by women who knew him that his attitude toward them was ever patronizing. Much of this can be traced to the robust social and religious traditions of the Poles. At a time when some priests in America would not touch a woman for any reason, Polish priests habitually offered a woman their hand in greeting. When the Poles got their freedom after World War I, women got the vote immediately. Kolbe was also devoted to a

---

*This must be an error; the magazine was not started until 1933.

strong mother. And he must have been influenced by his belief that the Virgin Mary, having been chosen by God to be the mother of His divine son, is the flower of the human race.

As a Franciscan in the 1920s, Kolbe certainly did not pal around with women. But, without ever overstepping the bounds of Polish Franciscan propriety, he was friendly. Beatification testimonies echo Polish laywoman Rosalia Kobla's* remarks that, while "he was a man of angelic purity—from his mouth I never heard an impure word—his conversation with women was as natural as it was modest." Sophia Roszkowska speaks comfortably of paying him a social call at the friary. His work with the nurse Anna Gibas at the Zakopane sanatorium indicates he was accepting of women as collaborators—again within the limits set by his Franciscan Rule. This is shown more clearly in testimony by his good friend Sister Felicitas Sulatycka:

> At the end of 1926, suffering from a recurrence of TB, Father Kolbe came to Zakopane, where I first saw him saying Mass in the chapel of the Sister Servants of the Heart of Jesus. I can't find words to picture the great devotion with which he celebrated Mass. All I can say is he gave the impression he was in direct touch with God. From seeing him say mass alone, I deduced his sanctity. I received Communion from his hand for many days before I got the courage to ask him after Mass if I could talk to him.
>
> He agreed, and for three months I had meetings with him. ["Above all, on these occasions," says Franciscan Giorgio Domanski, they spoke on the spiritual Militia."] At that time, Brother Julian said to me, "Only when Father dies will the world know who he was and the Order know what man he was among his sons." His Superior and doctors prohibited him from strenuous efforts or work in Zakopane, but every time he could instruct someone or go to give the sacraments he was always ready.
>
> One time, for instance, I told him about a member of [an active anti-Catholic organization] who was dying in a sanatorium. He responded, "I'll go to him." I looked at him as if I were in a stupor, since the man was an enemy of the Church. Father Maximilian replied that it was necessary to go to the aid of whoever has need of God.

---

*Listed in Beatification records as Koblowa, which means "wife of Kobla."

There was also a priest, Martin Szymanski, from Dydnie in the diocese of Tarnow, whom he used to visit. He was young, wanted to work, and found the thought of dying painful. One day, Father Kolbe gave him the sacraments and invited him to put himself under Mary's protection. After a few moments of indecision, Szymanski consented and found lasting peace. From then on until his death, he was totally reconciled to the will of God and even desired to die, saying to me, "Sister, just think. In a little while I'll see the Mother of God." It was by his sickbed that Father Kolbe received me into the M.I.

At this time in Zakopane there was great misery and poverty. I've seen Father surrounded by groups of children and poor people whom he used to aid with words and deeds. I thought then that he was the saint needed for our time, because of the way he manifested his love for God through love of his neighbor, forgetting himself completely.

After leaving Zakopane, I went back to Wirow, where I founded the M.I. in the teacher's seminary according to Father Kolbe's directions. One time the children there asked me if they could write to him, so I let them. In spite of all his work, he used to answer those letters. When I was teaching religion in a public school, the director said to me, "If all believers were like Father Maximilian, we could believe in God."

He and I were again in contact at Szymanow, where I was directing the M.I. I often invited him to give conferences, right up until the time of his last arrest. My invitations were in spite of the fact that he was not an outstanding preacher. He had no special gift of eloquence—only every now and then, speaking about Mary, he would become so fired he could speak with fervor and conviction. This happened most often when an audience was receptive. On the other hand, sometimes he faced people who didn't understand his ideals—who were looking for eloquence and philosophy. But he didn't let himself worry about this.

Many times I've seen him absorbed in profound adoration in our chapel. His whole soul showed in his eyes and his expression. I recall the sadness he showed when some priests complained a lot and showed too much preoccupation with material things. He used to say that he was afraid this type of thing would hurt his friars and weaken their Marian spirit. My superior, Sister Christina, one day said something about wanting to assist his friary materially. He replied that nothing is lacking to those who serve the Immaculata, but if anything were, it would be compensated for by the joy of serving her. Actually, they had their financial difficulties. . . .

Once I expressed to him my fear for the future of his works in case he didn't live. He reassured me that anything he had done was the work of the church and that Our Lord would continue his works.

By mid-1927, Brother Gabriel Sieminski recalls there was simply too little space available for the communications apostolate with its increasing amounts of equipment and new vocations at Grodno. Moreover, geographically the city was too isolated for a press apostolate. Finally, the group needed the freedom to act provided by a place of their own. Or, as Kolbe summed it up, the Grodno friary "walls had become too narrow." It was time for a move.

4

Niepokalanow:
The City of Mary

I N SEPTEMBER 1927, Janina Kowalska was living with her parents about forty kilometers west of Warsaw in a place known as Teresin. She remembers:

> One day a black car arrived in front of my parents' house. From it exited Father Maximilian Kolbe, his brother Alphonse, and four Brothers, among them Brother Zeno. They introduced themselves to my parents, saying they had come from Grodno to take possession of a piece of land given to them by Prince Drucki-Lubecki. They were going to build there. Since they had no place to stay, my parents offered them a room upstairs in our house and they stayed there for six weeks. My parents also fed them without any charge during this time. Father Maximilian was so grateful, he inserted in the Chronicle of the friary special mention of my parents' hospitality and instructions that the friars should never refuse them anything.
>
> I remember how uncomfortable Father Maximilian was anytime my mother wanted to serve him something special. He would give it right away to the Brothers. When my mother prepared a bed for him, he gave that to a Brother too and himself slept on a pile of wood shavings behind the stove.
>
> The first thing they erected on the bare land was a statue of the

Immaculata. Next, with the help of the neighborhood men who all volunteered assistance [according to Brother Zeno, these included not only Catholics but Jews and others as well], they put up a little wooden chapel where Father Maximilian said the first Mass, which I attended with my mother. Beside this little chapel they threw up a little shack in which there was a kitchen and several small cells for the friars. They put a wooden fence around all this, introduced the cloister,* and that was the beginning of Niepokalanow.

Niepokalanow: literally, it means "the property of Mary," or, in more modern language, Mary's city. John Dagis recalls the earliest days there, late in 1927:

We had to get those little buildings up quickly to cover the machinery and ourselves because winter was starting. We slept on the floors—it wasn't bare ground but wood planks. I didn't mind that. We were young, most of us, and strong. We saw how Father Kolbe sacrificed and never complained. So how could we? After all, he was older and sick, but he was eating everything we ate, doing everything we did, and sharing our lot completely. With a leader like that, it was easy to follow.

It may also have helped that they had been free not to come. Brother Gabriel relates:

Before the transfer from Grodno, he sincerely pictured to us collaborators the hard conditions we would be experiencing during this initial period and said we were free to follow him or to apply for posting to another monastery.

According to Janina Kowalska, "The new Franciscan chapel was really a great service to our area because it had been a long way to a church, and now we had a spiritual center right at hand." Their neighbors had been a big help to the friars as well. Besides housing them, feeding them, and helping with the rushed construction, even after the friary was officially open, its earliest meals were still provided by people like the Kowalskas. Even the first kitchen utensils were all loaned. An anonymous Brother pictures the initial meal at the friary:

---

* The designating of certain areas as out-of-bounds to those who are not members of a religious community, or to the opposite sex. At Niepokalanow, the church remained open to the whole neighborhood; the friars' cells, dining room, and work rooms, however, were off-limits to women according to Franciscan Rule.

Since we had no tables, when dinnertime came we put some planks across our suitcases and sat on the bare ground. After prayers, Father Maximilian, Father Alphonse, and fifteen of us Brothers sat at this poor table and partook of our food with Franciscan gaiety, rejoicing in what Providence had sent us.

By the end of 1929, two years later, there would be ninety-two aspirants, twenty-five novices, and twenty-five under simple vows eating in the tiny dining area. At mass, the doors of the chapel (which held no more than one hundred) would have to be left open, with some of the friars and neighbors standing outside. On the fields where carrots had been growing when the friars came would be more little huts. Brother Bart Kalucki, one of the 1929 newcomers, recalls:

> Father Kolbe always told us, "If after a bit you feel you don't fit in, that the life isn't right for you, just let us know. You're always free to leave. And remember, too: here one's effort is for others. If you don't feel that way, you really don't fit in." He said that, I recall, a lot of times.

Brother Lawrence Podwapinski, among the one out of three newcomers who stayed, tells what it was like to join Niepokalanow in its first wave of new members:

> I was twenty-six and the world belonged to me. My studies were over, I was relishing interesting work, and I was not short of girl friends. Then in April 1929, somebody gave me a copy of a Niepokalanow publication. There was an ad: "The gates of the city of Mary Immaculate are always open! Enter by those gates all young men who seek to serve Mary without counting the cost! In work without end, in abandoning self, in penance — this is the way to that peace which the world cannot give.
>
> "Whatever your skill, your trade or talent — there is room within the City's gate. If you can strive after poverty and heroic chastity in a spirit of humility — your place is here. In return — the joy of Paradise, of the vision of the eternal God."
>
> In spite of family opposition, I applied for admission. I don't have the letter I received from Father Maximilian, but in substance it said: "My dear child, you are accepted. Come as soon as you can. Don't worry about bringing a lot of luggage. You are more important than your possessions. So long as your desire is to serve God through Mary Immaculate, that's enough."

That same April, I alighted from the train by Niepokalanow. I remember vividly that, as I approached the gate, all I could see were some huts, looking like mushrooms on the open, marshy ground. Beside the gate was Our Lady's statue to welcome me. I knelt and asked her to accept my life in service.

With a smiling face, the Brother porter took me to Father Maximilian. I was struck by the simplicity of his room. It was small, no more than six feet by eight. The floor was bare boards and underneath the unpainted wooden bed was a washbasin. (Later we wanted to paint the bed or make the straw mattress a little more comfortable, but he wouldn't let us.) Father Maximilian himself was at a desk sitting on a backless wooden stool. He was working on a huge stack of papers. With a smile, he shook my hand and asked, "How are you, my child? I'm very pleased Mary Immaculate brought you here." Then he asked about my trip, saying I must be tired after the long journey. He suggested I have a good dinner and go straight to bed. While we were talking, there was a soft knock at the door. Another Brother entered, wearing mud-covered shoes. This was Brother Ernest come to tell Father something. His Superior gave him a very paternal smile and the business was over in a few minutes.

These first moments with Father Maximilian attracted and consoled me very much. They dispersed all the things I had heard in the world, such as that monks are very stiff and serious and always have to be focused on their death to come. The truth I saw was completely different — religious serving God with joy. . . .

The next morning I had my first meal in community. There were forty-two eating, only two of them priests. There was no tablecloth. Cheap tin plates and cups and a few loaves of bread were set out. After prayers we sat down (on stools or benches — all backless) in silence. One of the Brothers read something spiritual and two others busily served soup from a large pot. Our plates were soon emptied. After the meal, a short recreation period followed thanksgiving, then everyone got to work. Most of the Brothers were involved in publishing, with Father Alphonse as editor, but it was springtime, so the building department was also very busy under Father Maximilian's supervision.

After a few days, Father Maximilian asked me to prepare plans for the extension of the little chapel and to estimate the amounts of materials needed. About two weeks later, I was going to the lumber suppliers. Before leaving, I asked Father Maximilian for money for the trip. He opened a drawer of his desk and said, "Here, child, take whatever you want." Hearing this rather vague answer, I hesitated. Then Father Maximilian took a handful of money and, without counting it, put it into my hands. After my return I accounted for what I had spent, giving back what was left with some offerings I had received for our work. Father Maximilian opened the drawer and told me to drop the money in without counting it.

This gesture not only impressed me very much but, by it, Father Maximilian won my heart forever.

By the time it had become the world's largest friary, in 1938 or 1939, they would be keeping books—but always over Father Maximilian's objection. Prince Drucki-Lubecki, who came to see Kolbe whenever he was in the neighborhood to visit and play chess, relates:

> [Kolbe] wasn't interested in administrative details. His way was to rely on the Virgin Mary for everything. This way of handling things seems imprudent and I believe he was criticized for it by his Warsaw Superiors, but I don't state it myself as a criticism. Although I admit I tried to persuade him to adopt more businesslike methods, it looked like without them he always came out all right. I recall on my visits four or five times a year talking to the friars and hearing various ones say how often problems were solved as soon as they appeared. I remember one example someone mentioned: they needed someone with farm experience, and right away just that sort of person joined them. Kolbe had debts, I'm sure, especially in the beginning; but I think things got better as they went along. I know his philosophy was simply to rely on Mary's intercession and move ahead.

Kolbe, says the Prince—who was enormously wealthy before World War II—never asked him for a donation, nor did he ever drop in on his rich benefactor at the Prince's Warsaw residence.

That he did not cultivate rich, influential people such as the Prince is telling proof that he really believed that "the cash box of Divine Providence has no bottom," as he once told Brother Jerome Wierzba. Adds Father Isidore Kozbial, who was with him in 1929:

> He used to say debts were his wealth because they induced trust in the help of God through the Virgin. He was always an optimist and in the hardest times never faltered in courage.

There was only one hard rule: whatever came in must go into the work. Says Brother Lawrence:

> He often said it was fine — proper even — for us to live in shacks, to wear patched habits and mended shoes, so long as we spared no expense when it came to the most modern machines and devices to spread the message.

Father Anselm Kubit agrees:

> He was actually happiest when the greatest poverty reigned. He said a religious order must be a school for saints, so the monastery must radiate simplicity, penance, and poverty.

"God forbid," he told his old professor Dominic Stella, "that we ever try to make a profit here. Rather than that it would be better if the whole place burned down."

Janina Kowalska remembers that no sooner were the Franciscans moved in than, "although they were very straitened themselves, Father Maximilian organized meals for the poor." When the winter of 1928–1929 proved especially hard, the friars, still in their board shacks covered only with tarpaper or cardboard, distributed coal to the neighborhood poor. It was not just a case of giving *things,* Kowalska notes, explaining that Father Maximilian took time to make visits to the neighborhood sick and suffering. As the friars grew in number, some of them were assigned to work with the sick or the poor. Brother Mansuetus Marczewski, who was one of this group, recalls:

> In special talks to our group, he used to urge us to give alms with great delicacy so we wouldn't touch anyone's sore spot.

That sensitivity and intense empathy, which had replaced the rather tactless confrontations of the zealous young student in Rome, were perhaps why Kowalska reports, "No one was ever afraid of Father Maximilian. Everyone turned to him as to a father, confident that he would do his best to help them."

It also gives some hint as to why he had so many friends, from peasants to princes like Drucki-Lubecki, who recalls:

> I never heard him preach, knew him as a confessor, or anything like that. I came to visit him whenever I was at Teresin, spending three or four hours at a time with him because he attracted me. He radiated goodness. Everyone, I think, felt happy just to be with him, no matter

what one was doing. One felt he very rarely thought of himself — that he was always making renunciations. Nevertheless, he wasn't a sad, but a cheerful, man. I can't even tell you what his title was — whether he was editor, Superior, or what. He wasn't trying to be impressive. If a man ever existed . . . who had no pride, that was Father Maximilian. He was just like a child, and this appealed to me. We just used to play chess, eat, whatever, but he had a great influence on me. His friendship was a benediction.

Janina Kowalska came from an entirely different background than Drucki-Lubecki, but her feelings about Father Maximilian are not dissimilar:

When Father Maximilian and the other Franciscans were staying at our house, I served them their meals, and from that time until his final arrest I had frequent contact with him. He used to visit at our house and his mother used to stay with us on her trips from Cracow to see him. On those occasions, too, he would come over — particularly in the afternoons — and we would all visit. His mother used to tell me what a good and devout child he had been. She also mentioned a vision or dream he had in which the Virgin gave him two crowns. . . .

Additionally, we always went to the friary services. I've seen him during many masses and I can attest that no priest I've ever seen celebrated the way he did. I used also to talk with him afterwards.

From my own observation, I know he exerted himself enormously for human souls. He treated everybody with great goodness. He had no hesitation, either, about approaching people in the street or on a train and striking up a conversation with them on spiritual matters. Patiently and with wisdom he taught the little ones and the ignorant, while for the afflicted or downtrodden he always had words of comfort. Considering the friar's own poverty, he gave lavishly to the poor.

I often made my confession to him, and he was a confessor, as he was a preacher, of rare quality. As my spiritual director, he taught me to accept God's will and to place myself under the protection of the Virgin Mary. I owe him a lot.

There were also old schoolmates who came to visit, like Father Anselm Kubit, who had been with Kolbe in Lwow and Rome:

When I arrived one day, I went first to the poor, little chapel. In a few minutes Father Maximilian burst in through the sacristy door, unaware of me kneeling in the darkness by the back wall. I was able to observe how he prayed with his whole being. Knowing the primitive poverty in the life and living quarters of the place, the immensity of the labor, and the complete self-denial and then gazing upon the transfigured Father in prayer, I began to tremble. . . .

Those who have to live with someone around the clock know best if such apparent goodness is a shallow façade or the real thing. Representative of many Brothers' recollections are these comments by Brother Lawrence:

> I'm happy God permitted me to know him and work with him for so long. I have the most profound gratitude toward Father Maximilian, who formed my monastic spirit from that 1929 day he greeted me, first as my master of novices and later as my confessor and Superior.
>
> I've seen him accept without a murmur being corrected in the most conceited and obnoxious way by a Brother when he was the Friary Superior. I can also recall moments when external pressures got him all agitated. Then he would control his shaken nerves and from that moment show nothing through his demeanor. To me his life, as well as his teachings, which I often wrote down with scrupulous attention, constitutes a magnificent encouragement to monastic life. . . .
>
> I was not the only newcomer he greeted with warm interest. He had great personal concern for each candidate to the Order.
>
> As for his attitude toward the Brothers, I recall the night one of them was sick shortly after I arrived. I was still an aspirant and therefore wore civilian clothes rather than the Franciscan habit. Father Maximilian asked me if I would go to the neighbors, borrow a bicycle, and pedal to Sochaczew, a town fourteen kilometers away, for a doctor. When I returned much later (about one in the morning), he was still watching by the bed of the sick friar.
>
> In his own case, however, when he fell sick and some Brothers hung a sign on his door asking people to stay out and let him get some rest, he discovered the sign and handed it to someone saying, "Take this away, please; anybody can come to me any hour of the night or day *always:* I belong to them."

Brother Mansuetus, who met him in 1927 at Grodno, also remembers Kolbe's personal touch:

> It was late autumn. On a rainy day I was fixing a door. Father Maximilian noticed that I was lightly dressed. He called me right away and gave me his sweater, saying that he didn't need it. He did similar things for

many others. . . . I've had a lot of Superiors, but he was the best.

How did a man so committed to love of neighbor handle infractions of the Rule, personnel problems, and all the other burdens of a Superior? Brother Pelagius Poplawski talks about the Rule:

The characteristic trait of Father Maximilian was to admonish, to beg, to exhort — but not to punish. He succeeded in having all the friars willing to try to keep all the precepts of the Rule [only] because of his goodness and fatherly care.

Brother Mansuetus pictures Kolbe as personnel director:

If a friar couldn't handle his duties, Father Maximilian listened with kindness to his difficulties and took account of his problems. He was not just human but indulgent in such matters.

He also had a sense of humor: When Brother Gabriel complained one time too many about the food, he made him the cook. "He was another Saint Francis," John Dagis sums up. But if the love of poverty, charity, rapt prayer, and childlike simplicity that observers saw in Kolbe were all joyously Franciscan, in one area Kolbe parted company with his spiritual father. That was in regard to Brother Ass, as Francis disparagingly called his body. Kolbe had no desire to pass the boundary of self-denial into self-punishment, or climb to the heights of spirituality on the back of his broken body.* Brother Lawrence reports "a characteristic comment" he jotted down one day when Kolbe was giving a conference, as they were called.

Don't look for extraordinary mortifications, fastings, flagellations, chains, long prayers, or this sort of thing. It's enough [penance] to completely fulfill the will of the Immaculata — that is, the will of God — by being perfectly obedient. *was enough penance*

Brother Cyprian Grodzki adds that Kolbe obtained from the province-level Superiors exemption of all Niepokalanow Franciscans from the self-flagellation known as "taking the Discipline." According to Brother Pelagius Poplawski:

---

*It has been said that Kolbe's father, Julius, was very interested in physical fitness and every year used to race his sons barefoot through the first snowfall as part of his health-building program.

He was very concerned with our maintaining our physical health and made it a practice for the community to do morning gymnastics.

Brother Gabriel, who ended up as cook, says Father Maximilian wanted food that was poor and plain, but was very concerned that the diet be nourishing and health-giving as well. Brother Mansuetus remembers:

Even though he ate very little food himself, he urged us to eat well in order not to lose our strength. He often told us, "The car that isn't gassed up soon comes to a halt."

Finally, in a day when smoking was equated with masculinity and no one thought of it as a health problem, Kolbe not only outlawed it as an offense against monastic poverty but told some Franciscans in Assisi they should not smoke because it set others a bad example and it was bad for people's health.

As 1929 ended, a new Missionary Seminary stood on the friary grounds, headed by Father Alphonse. It was obvious that the friary was at the start of an even greater explosion in terms of vocations and apostolate. In the next year there would be 108 Brothers and aspirants plus 102 Missionary students. An electric generating plant would be installed, and other new structures would house expensive machinery. In a country of only thirty-one million, as many as 343,750 copies* of *The Knight* would be in circulation in a month, most to several-person families, while all sorts of new publications were on the drawing boards. The spiritual Militia itself, which had spread into other countries of Europe, was extremely successful in Poland, with 227,000 members. Finally, lest they lose their trust in Our Lady, as Kolbe put it, they were a staggering sum in debt.

If it was an exciting time, it certainly was also a time that demanded every ounce of Kolbe's innovation and leadership. Unfortunately, one person disagreed with that analysis. That was Kolbe, who always insisted Niepokalanow was not his, but Our Lady's, gift to God.

Leaving it in her hands, he was off to start another communication center on the far side of the world.

---

*December 1930 figure.

5

Japan

FATHER CORNEL CZUPRYK, Kolbe's immediate Superior in January 1930 and only four years his senior, was usually sympathetic to Kolbe's innovations. But Czupryk recalls:

> He came in before noon and asked me to permit him to go to the Orient. . . . I was taken aback.
> "Where will you live? What will you do?"
> "The Blessed Mother has her plan ready," was his answer.
> "Who'll take your place here?"
> He said his brother, whom I knew as a capable person and talented editor, would take his place. I told him I'd have to think it over, consult others, and then I'd decide. Those I consulted did not approve heartily. First he was ill, and second he didn't even know exactly where he was going. . . . Still, Father Maximilian had this gift: when he proposed anything, he did it so clearly, with such conviction and strong faith, that it was difficult for me to oppose his request. So in the end I agreed. I took the decision upon myself. I told him, however, to go by way of the Father General in Rome, convinced that there he would be sent back.

Father Orlini, another sympathizer, did not send Kolbe back; he only regretted, he told him, that he couldn't finance the trip.

"That's all right," Kolbe reassured him. "I've got my benefactors lined up."

Since he had no benefactors and abhorred lies, apparently he meant the three dead saints on whom he next paid courtesy calls, going first to Turin to an establishment known as The Little House of Divine Providence and the tomb of its founder Joseph Cottolengo (d. 1842; canonized four years after Kolbe's visit). The Pole had long ago made the Italian his treasurer—he used to keep his picture in the desk money drawer—based on Cottolengo's support of thousands of destitute and incurables relying only on what the providence of God sent day by day. His next call was at Lourdes, where the Church believed Mary appeared in 1858 to Bernadette Soubirous, a peasant girl as slow and uneducated as Kolbe was brilliant. In answer to the young girl's "Who are you?" the apparition had said, "I am the Immaculate Conception." Bernadette was another favorite of Kolbe's. From this great Marian shrine, no doubt he also begged Mary's favor. In Lisieux, France, was the childhood home, Carmelite convent, and tomb of Thérèse Martin (d. 1897), who had been canonized five years earlier, in 1925. Max had made a pact with her in his seminary days: He would pray for her canonization and from heaven she should take charge of the Militia's conquests. He only had three hours in Lisieux, but the avid chess player got off a postcard home noting that he had seen her childhood chess set, which "ought to bring some comfort to our obdurate players."

Early in March, he was on a mail steamer headed for the Orient. With him were Brother Severinus (who would later take back his given name, John Dagis), Brother Hilary, Brother Sigmund, and Brother Zeno, who remembers Kolbe inviting him to come, saying they might be martyred. The group ended eventually in Japan, after stops in Port Said, Saigon, Hong Kong, Shanghai, and other ports. China had been their first choice—they had even grown beards reverenced there, in order, Dagis says, not to be confused with European traders—but the Bishop would not have them. The Bishop of Nagasaki was not enthusiastic either—until he discovered Kolbe had two doctorates. He was in great need of a philosophy teacher for his seminary. Dagis says:

> As to publishing a magazine in Japanese, that the Bishop said was impossible until our group spent years learning the difficult language.

everything would then be done by hired translators

Other missionaries who wanted to publish hired Japanese typesetters and translators. No one believed Europeans could learn the language to the extent of setting type in it themselves. Only Father Kolbe had the idea that we should learn the language. That's how I came to be able to set type in Japanese, to the amazement of local printers. It was such an oddity that when I returned to Japan in 1973 for a visit, I was still remembered for my achievement. But the idea was all Father Maximilian's.

One month to the day, having arrived in the country penniless, friendless, and not knowing a word of the language, they were on the streets with 2,000 copies of the Japanese *Knight, Seibo no Kishi,* bowing politely and requesting people's calling cards. If you got a card you could send them a magazine; to send one without that implied permission would be a gross breach of etiquette. Eight thousand other hand-cranked copies were sent to parishes.

To put every penny into the work, they did without furniture, sleeping on the floor, and cooked, in one period, outdoors with only iron sheeting as a makeshift roof to keep rain or snow off the cook. The cook was, says Dagis, perhaps the worst hardship, with the food itself running a close second:

> To eat anything made by Brother Zeno, you had to be really hungry. And to save money he had us on mostly native foods — greens primarily — some of them pretty strange to Poles.

With their vegetables, another veteran recalls, Zeno fed the potato-loving Poles rice every day, telling them potatoes were too expensive. When a spud-starved Brother discovered they were cheap, the overworked Zeno snorted, "Rice doesn't have to be peeled— anyway, we only eat to keep alive, so what does it matter?" When later another Brother began cooking, they all cheered. Although he said nothing, they noticed the Japanese food was very hard on Kolbe, who, they suspected, had a sensitive stomach. So was the weather and inadequate housing Dagis describes as "in such bad shape that all the wind, rain, and snow came in on us—and stuck up on a hill, we got it all." In a letter home, Kolbe wrote:

> Heavy snow fell in the night. To sleep we had to cover our heads as the snow was hitting our faces. In the morning our dormitory was absolutely white . . . and the basins full of ice!

A Brother added:

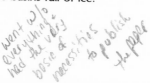

went on ... everything they had ... the busiest of cities to publish the paper

We're sleeping on straw . . . we eat from benches and sit on the ground. The poverty is extreme but we are very happy. . . .

When reinforcements arrived from Poland, this little group of Brothers brought a side of bacon, a glorious treat that was hung in the attic to be cut from on special feasts. One of the Brothers recalls:

One special day Brother Sergius went to the attic for bacon and found nothing. A few days later, after supper, Brother Mariano ran in shouting "A thief! A thief!" Everyone started for the attic. Father Kolbe wanted to climb the ladder but the seminarian Paul Nishiya stopped him, saying that was dangerous. So Father Kolbe tied his hat to the end of a stick and quietly raised it into the attic. By that time the thief was gone. At least they knew what had happened to the bacon. Father Kolbe smiled and said, "There are people even hungrier and poorer than we are."

His health was terrible during this time. Dr. Jacob Yasuro Fukahori recalls:

From his first days in Japan he had TB of the lungs so seriously that, seeing his X-rays, I was astonished. Sometimes he had a very high fever, chills, and shakes. Medically, TB's tremors are terrible. He might have fever for a week at a time, then it might go down for a month or two. During the worst spells he sometimes stayed in bed for short periods. But as soon as the tremors and fever diminished, he immediately got up and resumed working.

Physically he was very sensitive and reacted immediately. In temperament I'd say he was nervous* and passionate — the sort of person who has the capacity to become really angry, but he controlled his temperament very well.

I often tried to persuade him to go into a sanatorium and treat his condition all-out. He used to say that if he did, his condition wouldn't be cured; he preferred to work on as long as he could. And I have to admit that his health didn't narrow down his life. In general people with TB

---

*Because Dr. Yasuno wrote in Japanese, which was then put into Latin and later translated into English, it is difficult to discern whether he means "nervous" in the sense of "high strung" or "anxious." He is also, of course, evaluating a Pole by the standards of the Japanese culture, which is more controlled and less emotional.

tremors like his become delirious but I don't believe he ever did. I relate this to a sign of supernatural virtue.

Brother Bart recalls:

> When he couldn't get out of bed sometimes, the doctor would try to convince him to go to a hospital. Father Maximilian would say, "Give me a couple of days, I'll be okay."
>
> In the evenings, after a little group recreation time, we went to bed — worn out — about ten. Father Kolbe always said he'd stay up if anyone needed to talk to him. After awhile we noticed that Father, sick and the first one up in the morning, was being kept up till midnight or so every night. We Brothers then huddled and said, "Hey, let's cut this out so Father can get some rest," and we arranged the thing among ourselves. Father Kolbe had said nothing.

However, Brother Sergius, who had come out from Poland to join them, recalls a night when Kolbe thought he was dying:

> One night after ten he called me through the small window between our rooms to please come. He was sitting on his bed, dressed in his habit, suffering greatly as he repeated Our Lady's name. I felt his condition was very serious. He seemed afraid and said, "My son, please sit down." I did and he took my hand saying, "I'm not sure whether I can last out the night. I feel the blood in my head and my heart getting slower and weaker. If I have to leave this world, please tell the Brothers my last words were, 'Stick close to the Blessed Mother.' He told me several other things, his words spoken from the depth of suffering. I think he had had some kind of attack. I got very lonesome thinking he might die, and wanted to go call the other Brothers, but he didn't want that. Fortunately, as time went on, he grew calm, and by twelve midnight he said, "Our Lady has not called me yet," and fell asleep.

He wrote in a letter to Niepokalanow:

> I am scared of suffering and the thought of calamities . . . but even Jesus in the Garden of Gethsemane was afraid. This comforts me. . . .

In spite of his physical misery, in 1930 and 1933 he had to make trips back to Poland to attend Provincial Chapter meetings (gatherings of the Order's Superiors), at which the topics of discussion included debates over whether to shut his work down. He is described by Brother Lawrence as explaining as persuasively as possible why he wanted to continue, then sitting silently, his hidden hands busy with the rosary under his scapular, while they argued pro and con. Each time he not only won their surprised assent but permission for expansion—first, to found a friary, and the second time, to train Japanese who wanted to join them.

Father John Burdyszek recalls Kolbe's trip home in 1933:

> We young seminarians were very excited to see in the flesh our missionary with the long beard. The May day itself was glorious sunshine. Father Maximilian offered a thanksgiving Mass in the chapel he himself had helped to build. All the inhabitants of the City of Mary Immaculate, over four hundred, gathered together before the statue of the Immaculate Virgin outside the refectory. I could hardly hear his voice among the crowd. It showed his fatigue and debility after the long journey. He spoke as always, in the most simple words, as a father speaking to his children. He encouraged fraternal love: "Love one another, be humble of heart, do not be discouraged even by the sins committed in your weakness. . . .
>
> Blessing the electric power machine, he addressed it in the language of St. Francis: "Brother Motor! What ought I to wish him? To print well? I wish him to serve our Blessed Queen and Mother faithfully. Today he's blessed and takes the habit. Next he will be prepared; that will be his novitiate; then he will be put to work and that will be his profession of vows. What more shall I wish him? That he may work for a long time? That he may have plenty of companions? That he may be efficient? Ah, no! I wish him but one thing. That he may follow the desires of Our Lady. A good religious is good not because he does much, but because he obeys. So, Brother Motor, you will be a good religious machine if you do exactly what the Holy Virgin demands of you, whether it be to retire tomorrow or work one hundred years."

According to Father Florian Koziura, Kolbe "had always seen sufferings as a pledge of prosperity." The continuing threats of his fellow Franciscans to close the Japanese mission, and the hardships there, were not his only pledges: Japanese priest Father Charles Umeki recalls that when the friars arrived, he thought Kolbe's publishing plans "a joke." Bishop Hayasaka judged at the time "that they had taken the idea of trusting in Divine Providence to the point of abuse." The Bishop also admits he—and others—complained that the Franciscan magazine approached people too much on a feeling level, scandalizing the intellect.

John Dagis remembers the seminarian sent to finish his studies in Japan who quit and went to Brazil where, posing as a priest, he began collecting "money for Father Kolbe's mission" with which he lived high on the hog. Kolbe heard from angry Brazilian bishops who had to be convinced he was not involved.

Father Samuel Rosenbaiger, who eventually became head of the Japanese mission, recalls a whole slew of problems: There were loud complaints that the magazine resembled pagan religious publications too much. Priests worried that the Franciscans, so poorly clad and rumpled, demeaned the clergy as they roamed the streets seeking readers. The Apostolic Nuncio summoned Kolbe to Tokyo to read him out because he thought Kolbe didn't have Rome's permission for his presence. He did—red tape had held up the letter. Canadian Franciscans in Nagasaki argued that the Poles were muscling in on their territory and should be ousted. Even one of the Polish Franciscans made a scathing attack on Kolbe, who always referred to Mary very familiarly as "our mom" or "our little mother," with an article entitled: "The Virgin Mary—Mumsy? God the Father—Popsy?" (Ironically, in the 1980s, theologians stress that the Aramaic word *Abba* used by Jesus for God is one of the deepest affection, Daddy or Papa rather than a formal "Father"; so Kolbe's familiarity with Mary was perhaps merely another area where he was disconcertingly ahead of his time.) All his adversaries, Brother Zeno says, Kolbe answered with prayers. Handing the article to a Brother, he told him simply, "Read this and pray that a greater good comes out of it."

It would seem the hardest blow fell only nine months after the missionaries left Niepokalanow in the conscientious hands of Alphonse. News came that Kolbe's healthy younger brother had died suddenly of a ruptured appendix. Horrified himself, Dagis recalls that Father Maximilian showed neither despair nor concern that he should rush back to take up the Polish reins. His attitude when death took one of the Franciscans, says Brother Jerome Wierzba and others, was always "for us, death is a feast day, a cause for rejoicing," and he did not change his mind because the feast was for his brother. Only later did he recall poignantly to some Brothers how he had gone in to see Alphonse to say goodbye, found him asleep, and tiptoed out after kissing him lightly. Dagis recalls that, when the news came, they knelt and prayed. Then Kolbe told them cheerfully, unconsciously echoing Alphonse's last words, "Well, now we have a real advocate and friend in heaven; he'll be praying for us a lot."

And the facts, odd as they seem, show that the Polish friary, deprived of a very gifted leader and left with only the nervous Father Florian Koziura (who eventually had a breakdown) to guide it, continued its dizzying growth and even got out of debt, while in Japan the magazine that was so criticized—perhaps because it was so similar to non-Christian publications the Japanese could relate to it—reached a quick 18,000 circulation, surpassing every other Christian publication. And before eighteen months had passed, in May 1932, Kolbe was on his way to India to begin arrangements for opening a Christian communications center there.

From the Indian Ocean, he wrote a letter that makes it clear that the man who others later claimed saw their future still found his own obscure:

> I would like to be able to tear away the veil of the future and see where I shall end up, what results will be obtained. . . . I get discouraged; after which I see a ray of hope, etc.

He concludes that what he finds "very consoling and brings peace to the soul" is to remember that the work is for God. If God wills failure—so be it. It is enough to have offered himself, via Mary, to Him.

In a letter to Japan on his second trip to Poland, he praises one of the Brothers for a sacrifice made beautiful by the spirit of love in which it was done and urges them all to follow "Jesus' perfect example in this regard" as they offer small sufferings in love to their patron, the Blessed Mother. "It is not necessary," he says, "to seek them out. There are many things which afford the opportunity . . . something to hear, to see, to eat, to speak, to obey, etc. But be careful not to harm your health. . . ."

For him, one of those small sacrifices that did not harm health was to sleep on a hard straw mat. Brother Sergius was tidying Kolbe's room one day and shook the mattress to try to make it a little softer and more comfortable. Kolbe noticed and said, "Please leave it alone. It's my small sacrifice." Sergius kept shaking the mattress. "Why don't you obey?" Kolbe scolded. Sergius paused, then, moved by his pity for the sick priest, he went on. This time, he remembers, Kolbe said nothing.

Dagis pictures the feverish, exhausted Kolbe "pretending to us he felt fine," walking back and forth rosary in hand so as not to fall asleep while he struggled to fill the magazine's sixteen pages. He wrote copy in Latin, Italian, German, and French—whatever language a volunteer translator could work from. He learned to speak Japanese as did all the Brothers, says Dagis, each one teaching another newcomer (Dagis taught Brother Bart), but he never could write it well.

Bishop Hayasaka offered to sell them a vacant seminary but Kolbe refused, telling the Brothers, "It is better to invest in publications than buildings." Instead he bought cheap, hilly land outside Nagasaki. It was so steep, backbreaking labor was required to scrape out a flat pad for the first structure. When they did get a nice friary on the hill, no one would be able to see it because other hills blocked all view of the city. "Oh, the work!" moans Dagis, remembering. But when the atomic bomb leveled Nagasaki in 1945, speculation began that perhaps Kolbe's mystic's intuition played a part in his site selection. Hidden behind the hills, their premises intact and themselves uninjured, the Franciscans were able to take in hundreds of dazed orphans. (Although the Polish Franciscans had been treated very badly by the Japanese government during the war, they retaliated as Kolbe had taught them: they eventually made permanent quarters for one thousand children, the soul of this drive being simple Brother Zeno, already long venerated by the Japanese as a holy man.)

Dagis recalls:

Like another St. Francis, [Kolbe] loved cats and dogs—all animals—and flowers. When we got our own place, knowing how much he liked flowers, I said to him, "Well, now we've got plenty of room. You can have some flowers." But he only smiled and said, "I think souls will have to be my flowers." We were that poor. The same thing when someone gave us a dog. He loved the dog and, when it had puppies, right away he cried, "Quick, let's give her some milk and food so she won't suffer!" That was him all over. But in spite of his feeling for the dog, we were too poor. Our priorities, he said, had to be working for the people of Japan; so we had to give the dog back.

For a long time, the new place consisted only of about four or five rooms to live, produce, and print a magazine in. Sleeping conditions continued to be dreadful, this time consisting of straw mattresses in the attic where snow and rain blew in under the tiles. "We were so tired when we went to bed, we slept anyway," laughs Brother Bart. Summer, he adds, brought its own difficulties:

> The humidity was so intense that first you worked in your habit — that's all we had — soaked with sweat. Then when you washed the thing and hung it out, it wouldn't dry. We got used to it all, but some Brothers couldn't. . . .

In fact, of the first four, only Zeno and Dagis lasted. The other two had to return to Poland.

Father Cornel writes:

> Even the best Brothers — ones Father Kolbe himself selected — found it hard. The language . . . the long distance from Poland. . . . Some left the Order, others became ill and had to be sent home. The seminarians sent out so someone could eventually replace Father Maximilian had similar troubles. Four went. Only two lasted. With all this and Father Maximilian so ill, Father General made the decision to wind up the whole project.
>
> When I realized what was happening — that the mission into which Father Maximilian had put his heart and soul was to be closed, I had a conference with the General and Father Anselm Kubit, who had just been elected to replace me as Provincial Superior, and I asked to be sent out there.
>
> I was Kolbe's Superior and he worked under me. That period of time — three years — belongs to the most pleasant years of my superiorship. We agreed in everything, because Father Maximilian had that remarkably unique virtue of obedience. Naturally, there were differences of opinion, there was dialogue, but we always settled on something and God blessed it. . . .

A Brother who joined them in late 1931 recalls:

> Our new Superior left Father Kolbe in charge of the magazine and our spiritual direction. He himself campaigned to improve our health before, as he said, "you all end up in the cemetery." He marketed for cheap but nutritious foods such as pigs' feet, ears, and organs, and saw that they were cooked Polish style. He ordered less spent on the magazine's expansion and more on food. He insisted on a noon recess and a recreation period after supper. He was happy because he felt that, if not cured, [at least] Father Kolbe's health improved some.

The new Superior himself wrote home:

The Brothers . . . are full of the spirit of sacrifice. They willingly do anything they are asked. Fraternal charity too is remarkable. This is not because I taught them; . . . it is the result of Father Kolbe's direction.

The same Brother remembers Kolbe at recreation:

He was good [at chess] and played not just to please others, but to win. One night he had a skillful opponent. With his next move he was going to win. Then just as his turn was about to come up, someone intervened and advised the other player of a saving stratagem. This Brother, rather than be beaten, followed the advice and Father Kolbe lost the game. Then the disappointed Kolbe looked at the advisor with his sharp but gentle eyes and complained, "Why did you coach him?" Of course he wasn't mad but he was still regretting his near win.

Since he no longer had all the duties of Superior, although he was still overworked with his editorial work and teaching their Japanese seminarians,* Kolbe gave the Brothers teachings. He was always concerned to deepen their spiritual life, without which work and sacrifices become, he believed, meaningless. Dagis says:

He taught us theology, but he was so much more than a Th.D. in theology. He knew things, not just as rules or laws, but experientially. His aim was to penetrate the soul and see what could be done for that particular unique individual. Did he penetrate my soul? Ah, too much! I see him even today, fifty years later; when I walk or talk, he seems to be with me. I even dream about him all the time.

Brother Zeno, who says he felt from the time he first knew him at Grodno that Kolbe was "different from the others, a special person," adds:

He often talked about the Passion of Jesus Christ. . . . He considered himself unimportant and he used to persuade us too to consider ourselves very small before God.

It was just Kolbe's smallness and the Franciscans' abject poverty, several Japanese report, which drew them to the foreigners' help. Among these first collaborators were a Buddhist, a Protestant pastor, and a young man who describes himself as having been

---

*Kolbe's teaching at the local seminary (which had involved a long trip by street-car and a climb on foot up a steep hill) had ended, but the Franciscans now had their own seminary for local boys who wanted to join their Order.

simply "faithless." This workingman recalls he was recruited to help by a friend, and Kolbe, "even though I wasn't Catholic, treated me like one of the family, setting me to work alongside the Brothers." Dagis recalls the Protestant pastor Yamaki:

> A teacher, he loved St. Francis so much he had learned Italian just to read the Fioretti. A very intelligent and nice man. After a time he concluded that Catholicism was the ultimate form of Christianity. He announced this at his school and was fired.

Yamaki recalls Kolbe:

> [He was a] very gentle person who took great care of other religions' followers as well as his own. He had no prejudice toward me as a Protestant, always confided in me, and trusted me totally.

Yamaki also recounts that years later, when Kolbe was no longer in Japan, he received a letter from the Franciscan. At that time Yamaki had become a Catholic. He had had to leave his house (perhaps a parsonage) as a result, and was ill and impoverished. He says:

> As far as I know he had no knowledge of my situation, but he sent me a gift of money equal to nine months' salary saying, "This is some compensation from the Virgin Mary for the work you did without charge in Nagasaki."

Visitors also included not only individuals and curious Japanese families, but *bonzes.* These Buddhist priests posed for their photograph with Kolbe, who reciprocated by visiting their bonzery, where he was asked to speak to them on "this Mary Immaculate." Dagis says:

> Father Maximilian was a wonderful salesman for Christianity because he never pushed it. He never criticized or challenged any other religion. People would come and see us. They saw our life. They asked whatever questions they wanted and he answered—that was all. Like a good salesman, he let them see the product, gave them the information they asked for, and then left them strictly free to make up their own minds.

 To understand John Dagis's statement that Kolbe did not challenge or criticize other faiths as meaning that he was ecumenical in the present-day sense of the word would be incorrect. His writings make clear that he believed, as he had been taught, that all other faiths were incomplete or erroneous.* Thus intellectually he did challenge other doctrines. What John Dagis notes that distinguished Kolbe from his age—and ours as well—is that Kolbe never included in his war on a doctrine, war on its human followers. Them he approached as brothers, without attacking their beliefs. Instead he tried through love, example, dialogue, sacrifice, and prayer to lead them to the truth as he saw it.

How did his approach work? Apparently, very well. The Buddhist, the former Protestant, and the "faithless" young man all came forward to testify at the Beatification hearings years later. They had all—one eight years later—ended in Kolbe's church, and all believe he had a lot to do with their choice. They speak less of "salesmanship," however, and more of those things about Kolbe loved by Brother Henry Borodziej, who came out to Japan in 1932:

> [Kolbe's] enthusiasm had its impact. . . . [He] incorporated us into his activities fully . . . as he believed, so he acted. In spite of the fact that he himself was a highly educated individual, he treated everybody with love and without distinction of race, age, or education. Above all, I would say he lived for lay people. By means of his publications, he endeavored to get close to them, to reach every family. . . . He wanted to bring every individual to God.
>
> For me, personally, Father was a great man.

By 1936 when Father Cornel was packing to return to Europe for the next meeting of friary Superiors, he could prepare to report there were two priests and eighteen Polish Brothers along with a cleric, four Brothers, and eighteen seminarians who were Japanese or Korean. By 1939, these numbers would total seventy-eight men.

---

*Still, in an age when Protestants and Catholics routinely dismissed each other as "hellbound for false doctrine," Kolbe had the mystic's broader view. Although his spiritual Militia's charter speaks (in the language of the day) of converting heretics, Jews, Masons, and schismatics, Kolbe wanted to do this strictly by love, so that individuals might "freely choose" his faith, and he refused to believe that those who held other beliefs would suffer eternally for them. He felt God would give each individual the opportunity to know him, after death if not before. Thus individuals could only be eternally separated from God, he believed, by free, conscious choice, not by having been born into the "wrong religion" or holding "incorrect doctrine." Here too Kolbe anticipated present ideas. (See Ladislaus Boros, *Living in Hope* [New York: Doubleday/Image, 1973].)

The magazine, with 18,000 subscribers, had far outdistanced its competitors, now had a phenomenal circulation of 65,000.

Kolbe was happy. He would later reveal that in Japan, where he had suffered so much, he had received great mystical graces. The India foundation which he was working toward was for him only the next in a chain that should encircle the earth "until there are as many *Knights* printed as there are languages."

While Kolbe dreamed of putting the review out "from Beirut in Arabic, Syrian, Egyptian, Tunisian, Moroccan, Persian, and Hebrew," of setting up in Siberia, Peking and Shanghai in China, then moving on to Canada, the United States, the republics of Central America, Brazil, Argentina," Father Cornel worried over his friend's health. He writes:

> He was ailing badly. The hot climate and the dampness aggravated his condition. His lungs got so bad that in the hottest months — June, July, and August — he didn't leave the house. Often he was spitting blood. And still he did a lot of work, for we had a novitiate. He taught philosophy, too, and we had seminarians. [When he couldn't get up at all, he taught and handled correspondence from his bed.] Between the work and the climate, I knew he couldn't take it much longer.

With those successes and that fear, Father Cornel took Kolbe with him for the meeting in Poland. He did not tell Father Maximilian that he did not intend to let him return.

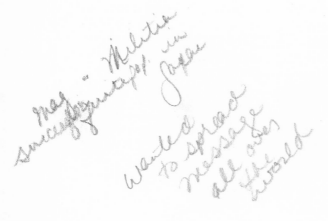

6

Poland, 1936–1939

R E-ELECTED A SUPERIOR, not of the Japanese, but of the Polish friary he had founded, Kolbe showed that his devotion to obedience was not just words. Without protesting that he had barely begun his world-girdling chain of communication centers, he headed back to Niepokalanow. At the friary, Brother Thaddeus Maj recalls, "With what joy we waited for his return!"

They also had a present. When Kolbe arrived, the Brothers who made the community's clothes, aware that he was sick and facing his first Polish winter in six years, presented him with a fur coat. Brother Vladimir Blaszczyk remembers:

> He asked, "Do the other Brothers have such fur coats? Certainly not; and for this reason, I don't want one for myself."

Disappointed, the Brother tailors did not give up: They made a warm, leather-lined jacket. When he inquired, they assured him that "the same type of jacket had been made for all the Niepokalanow sick," so he had to accept it.

Kolbe had been seriously sick when X-rayed in Japan. But, in spite of the heavier work of the much-larger Polish friary, when he was examined by friary physician Dr. Stanislaus Wasowicz, it was found that "he had old lesions caused by tuberculosis [but] these were no longer in need of treatment." Some of the Polish physician's other observations:

> I saw him about fifteen times over these three years, either because I was called to sick Brothers or directly to Father Kolbe. I examined him various times in my office or at the friary. Physically, he was diminutive and thin with a monastic beard and a lively temperament. As far as his mental health was concerned, he was normal to the maximum. He faced life with good equilibrium. One time I was called out at night to treat him — that was acute abdominal colic. During the course of treatment, I observed that he cared about his health in a prudent way without [either] the least irresponsibility or exaggerated concern.
>
> I also recall asking him once why there was so much evil in the world. He answered me that there are very few evil people, but that many do bad things out of thoughtlessness.

To reassure the Brothers about his health, Kolbe tried simply not to mention it or, as Brother Mansuetus Marczewski recalls:

> He would treat his infirmities or illnesses with humor. I recall when he joked about the patient who said, "Man must go to the doctor because the doctor must live; he must buy medicine so the pharmacist can live; but if he wants to live himself, he ignores the doctor and throws out the medicine."

Besides again getting used to Kolbe's insistence on strict equality between him and the Brothers in dress, the convent soon remembered he would not tolerate any other distinctions. Brother Vladimir recalls:

> One day he came to the friary barbershop and patiently took his place in the line of waiting Brothers. The Brother barber wanted to let him go first but he refused, saying, "We all work for the Immaculata and we're all in the same hurry."
>
> When Father Kolbe's turn came, the barber took from the closet his best cover, which he kept reserved for priests.
>
> "Put that away, my brother," his Superior protested energetically, "until the first one is torn. There must be no distinctions. All must have the same treatment."

A friary with its own full-time barber? Over what kind of establishment was Kolbe now Superior? Certainly it was a far cry from the little wooden chapel and shack with a fence thrown round them. In 1930, when he left, the place had already become an almost self-sufficient little town. By 1936, the friary had 694 inhabitants and more coming, although it still had no impressive buildings—just a lot more simple ones and a greatly enlarged chapel. Before the German invasion of 1939 halted its phenomenal growth, this largest friary in the world would have nearly eight hundred members with 622 Brothers and candidates, thirteen priests, 122 in the foreign missions seminary (down in the uncertain days of 1939 from a high of 186), and fifteen advanced students for the priesthood (down from fifty-six). Eleven publications would include a daily newspaper with a Sunday edition of 228,560 copies. In a country of no more than thirty-four million,* *The Knight* would have a 1938 pressrun of one million, with most copies going to households of several people. Brother Bart and others mention that these issues were further passed around the rural villages after subscribers finished with them. This meant coverage of a significant portion of the nation by the magazine alone. The spiritual Militia totaled 691,219 for Poland alone, with several hundred thousand other members in the rest of Europe, parts of the Far East, and other nations served by Conventual Franciscans. There were Brothers who did nothing but answer the mail (750,000 pieces in 1937 just from Poland). Brother Bart gives some details of the bustling city-friary:

> The place was going almost twenty-four hours a day — that is, we had shifts so some Brothers were working while others were sleeping.
>
> Father Kolbe was a very progressive man. He said, "If Jesus or St. Francis were alive now they'd use modern technology to reach the people." So before World War II Niepokalanow had a radio station, was preparing for television, had the daily paper, and so on. What went on the front page of that newspaper was discussed all over the country.
>
> It's true that in the Order before Father Kolbe, a Brother was someone who swept and cooked; Father Kolbe was so advanced in everything he seemed almost to see the future in the way he utilized people.

---

* The 1931 census put the population at 32.1 million, with 20.6 million describing themselves as Catholic; while the population estimate for January 1939 is 34.7 million.

He said, "The more you know, the better you can serve God." He believed in developing everyone's talents and skills to the maximum. I remember one Brother we had who became a watchmaker. He became known all over Europe as a master craftsman, and wrote several authoritative works on the subject.

This condensed article by Father Marian Wojcik, editor until 1939 of the Niepokalanow-produced daily newspaper, adds further details:

The assignment to the various departments was based on American tests of natural abilities. Each department had its own school. This schooling, based on the natural talents of the candidate, was so thorough that the Brothers quickly achieved professional level. One example: In the division of linotype setters, among thirty Brothers, four had the highest rating in Poland. Schooling was not restricted to training at Niepokalanow. Brothers who had greater talent were sent to Warsaw and Poznan. . . . [Father Wojcik himself was also sent abroad.]

Technologically, Niepokalanow was on a very high level. A number of inventions were later adopted by Polish industry, the most important, perhaps, being the electric automatic addressograph, which won first prize at the Poznan Trade Fair and later in Paris, and was patented in Poland and abroad.

Not only were houses built with timber from the sawmill and the inhabitants of the friary fed, clothed, and medically treated (there were a dentist's office, pharmacy, and small hospital), but even machines and their parts were manufactured. For instance, Brothers manufactured the extremely delicate plates for the addressograph, cast types, and so on.

Niepokalanow was one of the most modern printing houses in Poland, with three rotary presses. One could produce 60,000 copies an hour of the two-tone sixteen-page daily. Another enormous one printed *The Knight*, bound it, stitched it, and automatically dried it. That machine could do everything to make a 144-page booklet ready for use. The advanced engraving department could prepare a half-tone photographic plate for printing in fifteen minutes.

Father Maximilian, who had a passion for modern technology, was the soul of this technological development. In his plans for the future were building a papermill and an airfield to streamline service to our readers. In fact, when the war started, two Brothers were being trained as pilots in Warsaw.

There were also plans for publications for individual professions and population strata including weeklies for the different grammar and high school grades, a monthly for village bailiffs, publications for agriculture and handicrafts, and recreational literature including low cost, clean novels.

Brother Bart continues:

With so much going on and so many of us, there had to be organization. There were twelve divisions and some subdivisions. Among us Brothers were some who had a lot of education.* Those, and others with ability, he put in responsible posts such as heads of subdivisions and divisions. Every day a Brother collected each division's written report of their day's output.

These twelve divisions handled everything a city or a giant corporation might require from electricians, mechanics, and telephone workers in the Technical Division to shoemakers and health care personnel in the Material Needs Division to a group of priests and a Brother who provided religious education and spiritual care for both the night and the day shifts. There was even a fire department and—after sabotage—five nightwatchmen Brothers who patrolled the grounds with dogs. The sabotage, Brother Bart recalls, was linked to the Communists; other opponents kept the friary's newspapers off the nation's newsstands, so the Brothers built and set up their own. There were modern vehicles to transport them and, for moving around within the grounds, the community— which once had to borrow a bicycle to fetch a doctor—now had its own bicycle fleet.

With pleasure, Brother Bart remembers:

We used to see foreign bishops touring our friary. They were brought out by the Cardinal, who was proud to show what Poland had.

Diocesan priests, from whose ranks come most bishops and car-

---

*Giorgio Domanski, O.F.M. Conv., present head of the International Militia, thinks it important to emphasize that, although some of the Brothers were well educated, Kolbe managed to create a flourishing enterprise demanding technological expertise with men who, for the most part, had very little education. For example, Brother Zeno, one of his best helpers, raised in the Czarist portion of Poland, went only to a secret "patriotic" school, and this only in the winter. Zeno had only the most elementary knowledge of reading and writing.

dinals, do not take the vow of poverty required for all members of religious orders such as the Franciscans. Kolbe's old roommate Bronislaus Stryczny, still a very close friend, recalls both the visitors and Kolbe's intense devotion to this vow:

> If it was mealtime, Father Maximilian would always invite any guests to join us at the table. I recall the Cardinal from Cracow, deeply impressed, eating at the same poor table without a tablecloth and drinking milk from a tin cup.
>
> Father Maximilian loved the spirit of poverty and was faithful to it to the end. I used to come to his room with various business matters and never noticed a superfluous thing. Once, when I mentioned that such poverty might generate pride in thinking himself better than others, he just answered me with a brotherly smile.

If Bronislaus had a passing concern his old friend would become proud, it was because he thought him so gifted:

> In the management of such a powerful complex, Father Maximilian was extraordinarily precise and brilliant — an excellent organizer and wise personnel manager in the choice of his coworkers.

The techniques—round-the-clock shifts, high-powered tools, daily output reports—were borrowed from industry, but there were other things that kept Niepokalanow from being merely a religiously owned General Motors or Mitsubishi. As Brother Bart recalls:

> Father Kolbe was open to everybody's suggestions. In fact, there were suggestion boxes all around the friary. We also had community meetings, as well as division meetings, at which the best of these ideas were discussed and others brought up.

Explains Brother Juventyn Mlodozeniec, now stationed at Assisi:

> Because every Brother could contribute suggestions and plans for improvement, everyone felt responsible for his share in the total output.

Yet this could all still be a benignly run factory. A more crucial difference is noted by Brother Juventyn:

> The secret of our success was that, undergirding our modern organization of labor, Father Maximilian relied on supernatural obedience, which he himself practiced heroically.

Finally, the heart of the matter is summed up by Brother Bart:

> There was just a natural tendency to excel, because we all felt we were working for the glory of God.

Kolbe's devotion to poverty—obsession, some will call it—also made a difference. There is a natural tendency for fiery, young idealists to mellow into enjoying success, a phenomenon not unknown even in the Church. Businessman Eugene Srzednicki, administrator of Prince Drucki-Lubecki's estates, who knew Kolbe as early as 1927, recalls:

> I've seen Kolbe in the convent at Grodno in financial difficulties and I've seen him at Niepokalanow when [substantial] offerings were coming in. There was absolutely no difference in his behavior. He was always the same modest, simple Franciscan. In fact, when the money was pouring in, he himself was poorer than ever. Nothing for himself, everything for the cause. Not that he ever despised material things, but he used them only toward his goal.

Another important difference in the years of his physical presence was Kolbe's fatherliness. Father Bronislaus says:

> Although there were several hundred, father Maximilian knew each Brother and his needs. The door to his room was always open. For each he had a greeting, a fatherly smile, an inspiring word.

Brother Juventyn, accepted into the friary in July 1937 by Father Maximilian, "who impressed me greatly," remembers:

> After a week's stay at Niepokalanow I became ill and was taken to the infirmary. There I had more opportunity to become acquainted with Father Guardian, as we called him. There was not a day he did not visit the sick Brothers. We appreciated those visits greatly, for he had a certain extraordinary power of lifting up our spirits. Conversing, he shared his rich experiences with us, recounting impressions of his travels and his missionary work in Japan. Besides interesting anecdotes, he loved to joke. Especially at bedtime he liked to tell something humorous to invite laughter and cheer everyone up. But he also often reminded the sick that the little hospital was the most important workshop at Niepokalanow. Whenever Father Maximilian was away from the friary, the patients in the infirmary sorely missed him.
>
> My first work assignment was in the printery with platen machines.

When I was transferred to the night shift, Father Maximilian could visit me more frequently. He always greeted us with the name "Maria!" or "God Bless You!" and often he would ask us some question. Already I considered it an honor and even a special grace to have been asked by him about something. . . . There existed among the Brothers [too] the conviction that Father was an unusual person — a saint.

Although there was a general understanding that one could go to him if necessary any hour of the day and even the night, he also kept a time open in the afternoon, at which hour there stretched long waiting lines at his door. He would listen to each one with great patience. If the matter was pleasing, he would stroke his beard, smiling good-naturedly. . . . If the matter was not so pleasant, he would slip the beads of his rosary . . . praying silently.

Always soft-spoken, Father spoke slowly and deliberately, scanning the trusting client with his fatherly eye. In controversial matters, he would temper the ruffled feelings by asking for understanding and forgiveness. . . . [If] the discussion was too prolonged, he would pace . . . while listening intently and reflectively. If the problem seemed insoluble, he would kneel down along with the troubled friar to seek Our Lady's intercession. In this way, the decision arrived at seemed the best possible. Anyone who visits Father Maximilian's workroom should remember this: it is permeated with prayers, as its walls embraced the whole world and all those who have wrestled with their human nature [just as] Father Maximilian, with his fatherly heart, embraced all. . . .

That included those outside the friary. Father Vladimir Obidzinski, pastor of the Pawlowice parish within whose boundaries Niepokalanow lay, says there used to be a crowd of laypeople about Kolbe's friary confessional. He also says Kolbe used to accept invitations to come to Obidzinski's parish to preach, give conferences, and hear confessions—including the pastor's:

[I noticed] many poor go to the friary door. All exited well supplied. He saw in every man a brother in Christ worthy of respect and love.

In spite of his tremendous successes at Niepokalanow and the esteem of so many people (the postmaster told me Kolbe had friends and benefactors all over Poland), Father Maximilian was always so humble. He never took credit for anything, but all the good he did he attributed instead to the protection and help of the Mother of God.

Layman Casimir Debski remembers:

Once my baby fell sick, and in the middle of the night I came to the friary for Father Maximilian's help and advice. He came to me without a word about the lateness of the hour and with great solicitude gave me his help.

One did not always have to seek him out with one's troubles, recalls Brother Bart:

> Busy as he was, he'd notice a Brother seemed down and he'd call to him. A little chat and the Brother would come back to life. If you were open to Father Kolbe, he could always help you.
>
> I felt very close to him and I think — of course there must have been exceptions — that most of the Brothers did too.

How did those exceptions—the ones who by circumstances or temperament did not feel personally close to him*—feel about Maximilian Kolbe?

Stefan P. Wilk, M.D., a practicing physician in Los Angeles, lived at Niepokalanow as a junior seminarian from 1931 to 1935 when he was about fourteen. Since Kolbe was a missionary in Japan during that time and only home on visits, Dr. Wilk had no opportunity to become close to the priest—never went to him for confession or had private counseling with him. Dr. Wilk's view of Kolbe and Niepokalanow:

> I came to the monastery a poor boy glad for three regular meals, clean sheets once a week, and a chance for an education. Kolbe at that time was at Japan, but his personality permeated everything that went on at Niepokalanow. When he came back [on visits], it was as the great missionary who appealed to me in his soldierly aspect. We knew his goal was to raise up legions of spiritual soldiers and conquer the world for Christ through Mary. The whole monastery was like a military camp. Most of the brothers were young. They lived in big dormitories with just a box for each one's personal possessions. Because there were so many, the dining hall had to be used in three shifts.† The food was simple. For breakfast there was only coffee with milk, bread, and occa-

---

*This lack of closeness does not necessarily equate with lack of Franciscan vocation. Among the two or three who found that Niepokalanow was not their vocation were boys and men like veterinarian Ladislaw Lewkowicz, one of Kolbe's close friends at Auschwitz, who shared his ideals and loved him.

†This would have been necessary anyway, because of the round-the-clock work.

sionally some cheese. But it was nourishing. There were lots of sports. Each class also competed to see which one could say the most prayers. You counted yours and dropped them in your class's box. They were tallied monthly, but still there weren't long hours in chapel and nobody tormented us boys with lots of prayers. It was a very healthy place. Very well-disciplined. Not from rules, like a real military camp, but from religious obedience.

Niepokalanow was not a retreat from the world, as one might picture a Franciscan monastery. It was a beehive of activity. Kolbe was not interested in passive soldiers. What counted above all were deeds deeds deeds — how much you did to promote the mission. Everyone worked hard. As future missionaries, our job was to learn languages, math, chemistry, physics, etc. When I left the seminary and returned to regular high school, I found it a breeze.

Kolbe himself was a very fine mathematician and a man with a great flair for science. He himself did not teach any classes in the junior seminary, but he used to give lectures and talks to small groups of us. Mostly these were about Japan. I can still see him. He always had his hands under his Franciscan scapular and his head always tilted slightly to one side. Then he had this long, long beard. Whenever he greeted us it was with a big, cheerful smile.

But his personality was not what you would expect of a great leader. Although there was no doubt he was the spiritual head and spirit behind the whole monastery, in many ways he seemed just an ordinary Franciscan, quiet and shy and soft-spoken. And when he talked to us, his message was always extremely simplistic. I don't think he was simplistic, but the message was. He would speak very, very tenderly something like this: "My dear, dear Brothers, our dear little, little Mother, the Immaculate Mary, can do anything for us. We are her children. Turn to her. She will overcome everything." He spoke this way, not as one speaks of a spiritual personage, but like a son talking of a tenderly loved mother. This was always his message.

To me, in spite of the simplistic message, which I see as only the vehicle he used — as Buddhists and Hindus have theirs — and definitely not the most important thing at all, he epitomized greatness. He inspired a towering spiritual force. Certainly in his heart he was a soldier. If he had not become a priest he would have been a great general. He was a great leader. Not because he was a spellbinding orator. I've said he was not. Nor because he was an intellectual: He never gave us any big dogmatic discussions. Nor did he use political means. So under all these circumstances his leadership is remarkable. To me, what it consisted of was that in his particular time and place he knew how to inspire and mobilize many, many people to follow his ideals and do great deeds for them.

I just happen to be Catholic; however, I am also a broad-minded Christian. My present beliefs have evolved since my adolescence when I knew Maximilian Kolbe. Even if I were not a Catholic, or for that matter not even a Christian, I strongly believe that Maximilian Kolbe was a once-in-a-century great spiritual leader showing those of us who are Catholics or Christians of other denominations, believers or even non-believers, that those of us who have a spiritual force are beyond the reach of any tyranny, and are thus invincible.

I have seen the handwritten list of his goals from just before his ordination to the priesthood in 1918.* Number one was, "I wish to be a saint and a great saint." In this sense, like Gandhi, he was a fanatic—a man with an ideal that was his vehicle, his road to perfection—and he wanted to reach perfection. But Kolbe was also a down to earth, practical genius. For instance, he picked the site for Niepokalanow out in the middle of nowhere, and yet the place was at a crossroads of Poland as far as railroads and highways went. From the time he was thirteen or fourteen he spent all his years behind a monastery wall and yet, without ever having been exposed to mass communications, he knew how to use the press—and later the radio—to get his message out in a country not acquainted with these techniques. This shows enormous ingenuity.

Just imagine, into all these peasant homes in the southeastern part of Poland, where many couldn't read and many were so poor that their daily staple consisted of cabbage and potatoes all week long, here came—free—the first paper these families had ever received. And there was always an ad to "Become a Knight," not just a soldier, you see, but a soldier of nobility. Peasant boys formed a great portion of his army. Kolbe's greatness was that he knew how to inspire them—and all his troops—to follow his vision. And even more that he got the opportunity [in Auschwitz] to live what he preached and he took it.

For those who were close to Kolbe, what drew them increasingly in this period was something they call "holiness." Brother Felicis-

---

*This list was actually written in 1920.

simus Sztyk, who is still stationed at the Polish Niepokalanow, lived with Kolbe from October 1936 until the priest's arrest by the Gestapo in 1941. He says:

> I loved him as ardently as a child loves the best of fathers. At the same time I loved him with such great religious veneration that I sometimes had the desire to kneel before him as a living ikon of sanctity. Yet he was as natural and full of joy as a simple child. When he joined us for recreation or accompanied us on a walk, I was always closest to him [because] . . . I felt a need for his presence. Once when he was looking for me, he laughed to someone, "When I don't need him, he scampers after me like a calf after a cow — but now I can't find him."
>
> Why did I need to be near him? Because I felt holiness flow out of him as if it were a kind of unction from the other world.

Father Stryczny is only one of many who have exclaimed, "How extraordinary it seemed that Kolbe . . . was able to come up with spiritual help for so many Brothers, as well as lay persons and priests . . . and manage so many obligations." In the end, these observers all point to the intense inner life that Brother Felicissimus intuited as the source of Kolbe's energy and unfailing openness. Father Stryczny recalls:

> Despite his burdens, Father Maximilian was a man of profound and constant prayer. It was his custom to spend much time on his knees . . . [before] some important decision or [regarding] . . . some complex situation. Time and again he raised his eyes to the Immaculata, whose little statue stood on his desk. He loved the Immaculata and placed his confidence in her intercession to the point of recklessness.

Father Obidzinski remembers:

> On my visits to the friary, I was struck by how much he read the Scriptures. Any time I visited him I always saw the Bible open on his worktable.

Brother Luke Kuzba remembers:

> Several times a day he visited Jesus in the tabernacle. He said, "Here lies our strength — here is our source of sanctification." [The fruit of this intense spiritual life, this "vivid faith," as Brother Luke calls it], manifested itself by his constant joy. When things in Niepokalanow were going well, he rejoiced with all his heart with everyone and fervently thanked

the Immaculata for the graces received through her intercession. When things went badly he was still happy and used to say, "Why should we be sad? Doesn't the Immaculata, our little mother, know everything that's going on?" And in fact, Father Maximilian's life, notwithstanding his sufferings and many difficulties, was as if irradiated by a nimbus of joy.

At this period, Brother Luke speaks of Kolbe saying Mass so "full of grace" that "he appeared illuminated by an unearthly radiance" or, as Brother Cyprian Grodzki puts it more prosaically, "he underwent some sort of transformation when celebrating the holy sacrifice."

Whatever constant joy and transformations imply about Kolbe's interior life, they did not dull his perceptions. Father Cornel, who had been elected Superior at Poznan, recalls a visit to Niepokalanow:

> Father Maximilian had a map of Europe in his cell and was marking the places with little flags where he sent the monastery publications. Pausing for a moment, he said to me, "There will be a war. The boundary between Poland and Germany will be here." And he sketched the exact location of the boundary as it is today.

This could be a lucky guess, but since Poland's boundaries shifted rather dramatically, it is more likely the foreknowledge so typically a byproduct of the higher stages of mystical consciousness. Many astute observers, however, both sophisticated and simple, expected war. John Dagis recalls a Brother saying to him when Hitler first appeared on the scene, "If that man gets power, there will be a terrible war." Always a discerning observer of sociopolitical currents, Kolbe can be said to have seen war coming as early as 1936, then, without reference to his spirituality. Brilliant tactician that he was, he made his first priority upon his return to Niepokalanow not the technological advances at which he so excelled, but spiritual formation. Says Brother Cyprian:

> Dividing the friars into groups by categories, he gave each group a spiritual director and himself dedicated some months to increasing the Brothers' interior depths.

Themes of the conferences given during 1936–1939 show he desired to form as many souls as possible so deeply grounded in love that they would pray for those, who, he implied, would soon be persecuting them. In this he was correct. Eventually, almost all Niepokalanow's thirteen priests, many of the Brothers, and even some seminarians ended up in Dachau, Auschwitz, and other camps, as did Kolbe's brother, his cousin, and many other lay people he counted as his friends or members of his M.I.

To prepare souls, he used varied means. One was to emphasize the call to become saints. In 1937, in Rome for the twentieth anniversary of the M.I., he visited Quiricus Pignalberi, one of the seven founders and Franciscan Master of Novices at Piglio. In 1962, Pignalberi reminisced:

> He gave a little conference to the novices and, after having described for them the foundation of the Militia, he spoke of the need for all of us to be [spiritual] soldiers. . . . This is even more true for those who have joined religious orders, he told the young Franciscans. "A religious," he said "should be a synonym for saint." Then he encouraged them that sanctity isn't so hard. . . . It's the result of a very simple equation. And he wrote on the blackboard "V + v = S." The capital V, he said, is God's Will [he was using the Latin *Voluntas*]; the small v is your will. United they equal sanctity.

Another way in which Kolbe prepared his disciples was to give them something to remember—a spur to hope—in the difficult times ahead. Pignalberi mentions an occasion when he did this in Italy, and a number of Brothers have written accounts of what Kolbe said one evening when he announced that those who wanted could skip a long-anticipated entertainment and stay behind with him. About twenty did so.

To them, says Brother Thaddeus Maj, Kolbe explained he used this method so it would not be he who chose his hearers:

> He began, "My dear sons, right now I'm with you. You love me and I love you. But we can't expect I'll be here forever. I'll die and you'll stay. Before leaving, I want to give you something." [Then he began trying to share with them a mystical experience he had had in Japan, telling them he was doing so because] "greater difficulties and trials are coming from the hand of God for you—sufferings, temptations, and discouragements. For this reason, remembering [my experience] will lift up your souls, help you persevere in religious life, and encourage you in the sacrifices [God through] the Virgin Mary asks of you."

Unfortunately, a lifetime of trying to become modest and humble had succeeded so well that he couldn't bring himself to give them any details and ended instead by telling them not to desire extraordinary experiences. All that he actually revealed about the experience was that heaven had been promised him with absolute certainty. Since everyone there would have said that if Kolbe wasn't going to heaven, no one was, this could not have been exactly a shattering revelation.

However, he did corroborate the interior joy that Brother Luke, Brother Felicissimus, and others thought they saw in him.

"Dear sons!" he said. "If you only knew how happy I am! My heart is full of that peace and joy which can be experienced even here on earth. Yes, in spite of the anxieties and worries of each day, at the bottom of my heart is always a peace and joy I can't describe."

Brother Cyprian recalls:

The joy that shone in Father's face and the tears in his eyes communicated his emotion to us all. Later — after his death — we said among ourselves, we who were there, that it had been like a Last Supper. . . .

Brother Benevenuto Stryjewski notes:

It seemed that in his thoughts he flew ahead in time and saw clearly the future. . . . [He] tried to make the most of his time — notwithstanding so many occupations and difficulties that weighed on him as Superior — to prepare us. . . .

During this period it was said that just being with him was a spur to spirituality. Seminarians told each other, "Let's go see the saint," and even a priest such as Francesco Giusta, secretary for the Franciscans' missions, recalled with something like awe accompanying Kolbe to visit a distinguished and saintly theologian:

I spoke very little because I felt myself very small stuff in comparison to the two confreres, especially before Father Maximilian, whose words, peaceful and mellow-voiced, showed great delight [as he] . . . spoke on Mary's active participation in the life of the mystical body. . . . There was nothing ostentatious or artificial in his words; rather, he spoke with the simplicity of a child and at the same time with the certainty of a man inspired.

My wonderment, already great by what I heard, grew as my eyes took in the expression of his face. It was illuminated from time to time by an enchanting serene smile, quasi-physical manifestation of the intimate mystical joy of one who, while still on earth, feels rapt by the view of some heavenly beauty. And meantime his expression, habitually sweet and profound, was lit by a strong light [*lampeggiava di vivissima luce*].

To prepare his sons for the coming conflict, he was continuing his custom of giving spiritual conferences at least twice a week as well as on Sundays.* In these—often, Brother Pelagius Poplawski recalls, using the scripture, "The just man lives by faith" as a theme—he spoke on how to use suffering to benefit oneself and others; how to rejoice in spite of sufferings and trials and, even in them, how to remain free—and hence fearless—in any circumstances; and the importance of loving and praying for one's persecutors, even one's torturers and murderers.

From conferences given in the first half of 1938, various listeners recall the following statements:

> "My sons, a frightful struggle threatens. We don't know yet what will be its details. But here, in Poland, we must expect the worst."
>
> "War is much nearer than one can imagine" [this was in May], "and if war comes, that means the dispersion of our community. We needn't get worried, just bravely conform our wills to the will of Mary Immaculate."
>
> "In a sense we can even enjoy the present situation because, through these difficulties, we encourage each other to greater zeal and realize more clearly our need for prayer and penance."
>
> "Whatever happens, everything will be for our good. We are in such a position that nothing can do us any harm. The moral and physical sufferings will only help towards our sanctification. . . . We ought even to thank our torturers and show our gratitude to them by obtaining, through Mary Immaculate, the grace of their conversion. In short, we are invincible!"

On May 14 of that year, when Niepokalanow was at the height of its successes and immensely influential through its periodicals and daily paper, and while Kolbe himself was making plans for

---

*A collection of his conferences, not available in English, fills 458 pages.

film production, the new airstrip, and so on, Brother Lawrence Podwapinski wrote in his conference notes:

> Father told us in today's conference that Niepokalanow's success is not based on material expansion but on the deepening of charity in our souls. The true development of Niepokalanow is the development of God's love in our hearts. . . .
>
> Even though the friary declines materially, as long as our souls advance . . . Niepokalanow is developing. Even if they disperse us and all are obliged to flee deprived of their habits, if love is growing in our souls, then Niepokalanow, I repeat, is progressing.

Though written in 1932 for his spiritual soldiers of the far-flung Militia, an article titled "Our War" sums up the message that consumed so much of Kolbe's energy between 1936 and 1939. In it he says:

(1) Don't set out to do your own works for God, however great these might be, but give yourself humbly into his hands to do his works. (2) Accept all that happens as his will, including the sufferings he permits (not causes) you to undergo at the hands of evil men, knowing that even these will mysteriously enrich you. (3) As members of the spiritual army fighting under the generalship of Mary, give yourself to God through service to her. To be one in will with Mary of the great fiat, the only human being whose will has never deviated by her choice from God's, is to be perfectly united to the will of God. And it is this alignment of your will with his that is the pressing business of your life. (4) Offering yourself totally to God, let him transform you into a knight of love who, with others, will conquer the whole world, not in the sense of capturing it, but of freeing it.

He ends this article by saying that when each Militia member is "set aflame with the fire of divine love (I repeat we are not talking here of sweet tears and feelings, but of the will) . . . melted (and) fused to God . . . we will melt the whole world and each individual in it with love."

Hitler's conquests began with the annexation of Austria and dismemberment of Czechoslovakia. Brother Rufinus Majdan remembers:

> When the Germans occupied Czechoslovakia in 1939, we wanted to

headline the story, "Czechs Greet Germans with Hatred"; but Father Maximilian saw it and ordered a change. He said it was never right to encourage hatred.

As those words were spoken, Hitler's and Stalin's emissaries were shaking hands on their secret pact for the dual invasion of Poland.

7

War

I N AUGUST 1939, Hitler's panzers were poised for the Blitzkrieg (lightning strike) into Poland. Brother Juventyn recalls those days at the friary:

> Air-raid alarm signals were installed at Niepokalanow. When the siren sounded, all the buildings and lighted places had to be blacked out immediately. During one such practice alarm we were having a choir rehearsal and did not hear the warning signal; our room was not darkened. Suddenly, the door flew open, Father Maximilian ran in breathlessly, and exclaimed in a loud voice, "How can you disregard the drill?" Quickly, however, he calmed himself and bid us good night. It impressed us immensely that he could control himself in such a critical situation.

Germany invaded Poland on September 1, 1939. Brother Juventyn remembers the strained silence at the monastery as the printing presses stopped on September 5 and even construction work on the church halted.

> Father Kolbe, like a loving father, had for some time been preparing us for those trying days. On August 28, he spoke to us on the three

stages of life: first stage, the preparation for activity; the second, activity itself; third, suffering. He said:

"The third stage of life, the one of suffering, I think will be my lot shortly. But by whom, where, how, and in what form this suffering will come is still unknown. However, I'd like to suffer and die in a knightly manner, even to the shedding of the last drop of my blood in order to hasten the day of gaining the whole world for God through the Immaculate Mother. I wish the same for you as for myself. What nobler thing can I wish you, my dear sons? If I knew something better, I'd wish it for you, but I don't. According to St. John [15:13] Christ Himself said, 'Greater love than this no one has, than to lay down his life for his friends.'"

Located between major rail lines and the important Poznan-Warsaw highway, the friary lay waiting Hitler's bombers. On September 5, by order of the civil authorities, the dispersion so often spoken of by Father Maximilian became a reality. Almost all the 622 Brothers, 137 seminarians,* and thirteen priests on the 1939 friary roster who were at Niepokalanow left for what was hoped would be safer areas. Brother Ferdinandus Kasz recalls that when Kolbe bid the young Franciscan Brothers goodbye, to safeguard their vocations he cautioned them against drinking, smoking, or adopting nonclerical haircuts. Brother Juventyn was among the listeners at Kolbe's last brief conference before the dispersal. Urging all to seek the intercession of Mary, who "will certainly lead you safely through all difficulties"—by which undoubtedly he meant keep them faithful to love, not spare them suffering—he also said, "Many of you will not return to Niepokalanow. I myself will not survive this war." Almost all went home to their families. Some, on Kolbe's advice, attached themselves to the Polish Red Cross. A few fled the country or went at once into hiding because they were known to be on Gestapo lists for immediate arrest. Prince John Drucki-Lubecki recalls:

I left Poland on September 19, 1939. The Franciscan Provincial in Warsaw asked us to take the editors of the Niepokalanow newspaper, the Maly Dziennik [Little Daily], with us when we left. They were the most vulnerable—not because their opposition against the Nazis was unusual or virulent—we Poles were all against the Nazis as a matter of principle.

---

* Some students had not yet returned from their summer break.

The paper actually was not a political paper but, naturally, had been critical of the pagan Nazi ideology. It was well-written, objective. . . . Its director was Father Marian Wojcik.

Kolbe himself rushed by auto to Warsaw, not yet fallen to the Nazis, to get orders from the Province-level Superior. Other priests were present at their meeting.

From the tone of his conversation, we understood that Father Maximilian, too, was thinking of leaving Niepokalanow for a safer place. Then Father Felix Wilk, Superior of the Warsaw friary, proposed to Father Provincial that he order Kolbe to remain at Niepokalanow without regard for the consequences for the good of the friary. The Provincial gave this order and, without a word of protest, Father Kolbe accepted it. That same day he returned to Niepokalanow.

Brother Rufinus Majdan remarks:

He was acting out of obedience. He was aware of the threats to his safety.

On his return Kolbe found between thirty-four and thirty-eight Brothers and a couple of priests, including Father Pius Bartosik, whom he had indicated at the "last supper" as his chosen successor. Brother Juventyn, who was also one of the group, says:

How grateful Father Maximilian was when we expressed our willingness to remain with him unconditionally to the end.

On September 7, we experienced our first air raid. Enemy planes were hurling bombs on Niepokalanow and the neighborhood. Father Kolbe was running between the buildings from one . . . to the other, comforting and raising our spirits.

Perhaps in these hours the friary collected part of its reward for never having sunk any money in imposing buildings. At any rate Father Maximilian noted that only four minor-caliber bombs hit Niepokalanow, with the only damage being a new door. Not a single person was injured. This was not the case outside the friary, however. Brother Ferdinandus Kasz recalls:

There were many wounded in the neighborhood, so Father set up a hospital in the convent, where we cared for them.

One of the two priests, Father Florian Koziura, remembers gratefully:

> He saw how nervous the bombardment made me and sent me to Warsaw. I admired his own tranquility and peace as he remained at his post.

On September 12, the Polish defense line collapsed and retreating Polish forces left several seriously wounded soldiers and officers with the friars. Brother Juventyn's account continues:

> As our armies retreated to Warsaw for a final defense, Father Kolbe, vested in a chasuble bearing the inscription "Regina Poloniae, ora pro nobis!" ["Queen of Poland, pray for us!"], celebrated Mass for our endangered country, its defenders, and Warsaw in particular.

The friars waited nervously for the German infantry to arrive on their doorstep, not knowing whether the invaders would ignore the Franciscans, imprison them, or simply shoot them. Brother Juventyn recalls:

> In Niepokalanow, as for all people in Poland, these were days of suffering and terror. The shock experienced by the defeat on the battlefront, the prospect of the loss of freedom, the bombardment, and the uncertainty of what the invader would do — all this was a terrible psychological trial for everyone. . . . Every day during our morning meditation, Father Maximilian reminded us that this might be the last day of our life and tried to prepare us for a holy death.

On September 19, the Germans arrived. They placed everyone under arrest. Brother Juventyn kept a sort of diary in a notebook.

> Upon Father Kolbe's earnest entreaties, the German soldiers permitted two Brothers to stay behind to tend to the wounded soldiers. So Father appointed Brother Witold Garlo as head infirmarian, and turning to Brother Cyriak Szubinski, he pleaded, "Son, stay and take care of the sick." We all begged Father Kolbe to stay behind, but he refused, saying "I'm going with you."

When Brother Cyriak balked, Kolbe humbly reassured him, "You'll be more useful than I would." As they were led to trucks, not knowing their destination, Father Maximilian was serene, even cheerful, reminding his troops that they, too, were on a mission. With his irrepressible good humor, he pointed out how lucky they were to have the Germans provide their transportation without it costing them a penny. Trucked to Rawa Mazowiecka, they spent the night there in a church commandeered by the Germans from the Passionist Fathers. In the morning, neighborhood women pestered the guards until they were permitted to provide the prisoners with food. That day, Brother Juventyn remembers:

> They trucked us to Czestochowa. What joy filled our hearts when the trucks stopped in the alley of the Blessed Virgin Mary, from where we could see plainly the steeple of the Monastery of Jasnagora. There we offered the fate of our martyred fatherland to the Queen of Poland.
>
> The neighboring people rushed at once to our assistance. The more daring even came to the cars to give us food. At first the soldiers did not object, but later they refused such offers. Then the good people of Czestochowa began to throw to us rolls, cookies, and candy. Some even suggested escape, offering us civilian clothing. Realizing the trend of the suggestions, the Germans ordered instant departure. . . .

As part of a group of about six hundred prisoners, they were put on a train for Lamsdorf (present-day Lambinowice), and after two days there for Amtitz (present-day Gebice) in Germany. They boarded singing a hymn. Brother Cyprian Grodzki recalls:

> Father Maximilian told us that maybe the Immaculata wanted to use us to found a new Niepokalanow in Germany.

Brother Juventyn's reminiscences continue:

> During that trip, one of our brothers became ill. Father Maximilian asked us to prepare more comfortable bedding for him. So the good brothers willingly offered their coats, and Father Maximilian himself looked after the patient. During one stop at the station, we called through the small window to one of the German railroad men to give us some water for the sick man, because there was a pump with the sign "Trinkwasser." They turned to us with a fierce look. One of them shouted, "Don't give them any water. Let them die, Polish swine!"
>
> At another station, we repeated our request for water to a traffic agent. Gentlemanly and cultured, he opened the door of our coach and even permitted us to leave for a while. For the sick person, he brought some coffee and some cookies.

That evening they stopped in sight of a water fountain. A soldier was willing to hand them water but, as he raised it to the window, it was snatched away, Brother Juventyn recalls, by someone who snarled, "They're all destined for extermination."

Sunday, September 24, they arrived in Amtitz, an internment camp of tents grouped in areas separated from each other by barbed wire. Double barbed wire fenced the total enclosure and sentries in watchtowers kept machine guns at the ready. The Germans who ran the camp were very hostile to the Poles, who arrived branded by the soldiers who had guarded them as "Polnische Banditen" who gouged out the eyes of Germans.

> Father Maximilian felt this injustice most keenly and, during our trip, he wanted to explain to the soldiers that their false and hostile propaganda was harming our people very seriously. But he found no suitable occasion. . . .
>
> The director of our tent was Sergeant Sturn, a worthy and kindly Protestant from Berlin. From the very beginning of our stay at Amtitz, Father Maximilian tried to win him and dispose him more favorably toward the Poles. He asked our prayers for this intention and himself prayed fervently, seeking an occasion to meet him. . . . Brother Telesfor Bobrycki introduced Father Maximilian to Sergeant Sturn. After that, we frequently saw them conversing. Not long after, the ice of indifference and prejudice of the Germans toward the Poles began to thaw. Sergeant Sturn favored Father Maximilian with special respect and goodwill.

On his part, Father Maximilian showed genuine goodwill to Sturn and every human being. If he suffered to see German hatred of the Poles, he suffered equally when the Polish victims hated the oppressors. All who were with him during the war state unequivocally that Maximilian Kolbe never showed the slightest dislike for the Germans. A man of peace, his was the conciliation founded on courage, not fear. Several witnesses recall his fearlessness in Amtitz about defending Christianity's ideals and commandments. Brother Jerome Wierzba says:

> In the camp he always courageously intervened with the German authorities when we were robbed. . . . I also one time saw him act in complete indignation. I have to explain how remarkable this was. I remember even back before the war, when Brother Evodius was speeding and had an accident with the car. We needed the car badly and the damage was extensive. In fact, the repairs took months. Father Maximil-

ian came to the place of the disaster. All he said to Brother Evodius was, "Now don't worry. Don't be upset." He showed absolutely no irritation or even worry over the matter. But in Amtitz I recall when a prisoner expressed himself indecently about his own mother, Father was so indignant that the man calmed himself and shut up.

Brother Cyprian adds:

> I was there, too, in that mass of ten thousand internees. It was a prisoner from the lowest classes who became so angry during the distribution of food that he began cursing his own mother. Father Maximilian, with an indignation very unusual for him, stamped his foot and exclaimed a number of times, "You're not allowed to malign your mother."

A similar incident was witnessed by farmer Stanislaus Pokropek, who was arrested by the Germans for no particular reason while cultivating his fields. He lived near Kolbe for a month at Amtitz, and regarded him "as a great example to the rest of us." Pokropek says:

> I have a particularly good memory of the day two prisoners started fighting. One made some remarks about the other fellow's mother. Father Kolbe at once approached the adversaries. He seemed deeply stirred as he said, "That's no way to talk of motherhood." I can't recall the other particulars of what he said as he ordered them not to talk that way, but I know the fight suddenly stopped and never recurred.

Nor were the friars exempt, as fellow prisoner Brother Ferdinandus Kasz recalls:

> One of our ex-friars, in Amtitz known as Brother Dionigi Molga, told me later that in 1939 he swiped an entire bucket of soup from the camp kitchen. Father Maximilian told him this was unjust to the other prisoners and ordered him to divide the stolen soup among them all.

Many would have said Kolbe was crazy, since the food was at near starvation levels.* But where he asked others to walk, Kolbe

---

*According to Brother Juventyn, "At the camp, breakfast consisted of black coffee or soup whitened with milk. Dinner was one-half quart of soup with a few floating bits of potatoes, cabbage, carrots, or turnips, but without any fat. Black, unsweetened coffee, or soup made of flour sifted into boiling water was all we had for supper. A whole potato was a rare treat. One half pound of bread was the main food of the day. With such meals, one's legs refused to carry a person. . . ."

always led himself. Brother Rufinus Majdan recalled a day when Father Maximilian distributed his entire daily ration to others. Brother Juventyn says whenever Father Maximilian noticed a Brother suffering from hunger, he shared his bread with him. And Brother Jerome's reminiscences note that when Father Maximilian received a box of cheese for himself from the camp kitchen, he insisted on sharing it with them all. Jerome's portrait of his spiritual father:

> He was totally enamored of God. When in the camp we suffered hunger, cold, and when we slept on the ground or on hay under tents — and it was already a snowy and icy November — and we had no water to drink, and while we hadn't changed our underwear for three months, and while the insects and filth tormented us, Father Maximilian bore it all with joy. It was a way, he felt, he could show his love for God. It was at this time that I wrote down his statement that a certain sadness pervades even fervent souls when they realize that in heaven they will no longer be able to show God their love by suffering for him. Brother Pelagius made note of another remark: "The man who avoids suffering doesn't know what happiness is." I also recall from his talks that he longed to die and be united to God. In the camp we couldn't have Mass, but even there I recalled how, when he received Communion or distributed it to us, the holiness and union with God that showed in his face was unlike that of any priest I have ever known. He kept trying to teach us that the essence of sanctity consists of our will being one with the will of God. For that reason, he advised us before we acted to ask the Virgin Mary — whose will is always one with God's — what she would do in the situation and to then proceed as our conscience directed. He prayed a lot with us, gave conferences, and organized spiritual retreats. With us, he also organized services in which the lay prisoners participated and he heard their confessions. He took the entire experience of imprisonment with serenity and submission to God's will. There was only one thing about him that annoyed me: he seemed to repeat too often and too insistently that we would be freed soon and that the Immaculata's help would be involved. This irritated me. For others, his remarks strengthened their hope.

Brother Juraszek recalls:

> For a while I slept by him. I awoke during the night once, suddenly

aware that someone was very gently tucking in my feet. I opened my eyes — and what did I see? It was Father Maximilian who was covering my feet so tenderly. Every time I recall this incident, tears well up. He seemed to me then as infinitely good and tender as the best mother. After this, I also noticed that he was secretly giving a large part of his ration of bread to a friar who suffered from hunger more than the rest of us. And our rations were so small that only could one with the largest heart deprive himself of any part of them.

Brother Juventyn remembers a special occasion:

On the evening of October 12, Father Maximilian's feast day, after the lay people went to bed, we gathered at the entrance of the tent. But on that evening he was walking outdoors and praying longer than usual. When he finally came in we surrounded him, singing the traditional "Plurimos annos." Father Pius Bartosik extended greetings to Father Maximilian on his feast day in the name of all and so did Michael Miczko, a cleric.

Father Maximilian, looking at all of us with love, said tenderly, "My dear sons, I was thinking of what I can give you for my feast day. I have nothing. But let me share with you my wish that you entrust yourselves more completely to the Immaculata. In the midst of today's trials, let's submit ourselves to the will of God. When suffering is remote, we're willing to do anything. Now that it's here, let's accept it and bear it willingly to gain as many souls as possible. . . ."

Words, however, were inadequate to express his love. So he broke the piece of bread he had and shared it with all of us. . . .

Brother Juventyn also recalls:

One day at Amtitz Father Maximilian prophesied about the future of Poland, emphasizing his statement by striking his cane against the ground: "Dear children, you will see that even here there will be a Poland." [Today Amtitz, known as Gebice, is in Poland.*]

Protected only by a tent against the late-year cold, tormented by lice, and giving away part of his inadequate rations, the tubercular Franciscan, Brother Juventyn says, "remained quite well." When

---

* Too small to be found on most maps, it is in Krosno County on the Odra River, near the German border.

they were moved and came under a new German officer, this time a Catholic of Polish descent, Father Maximilian quickly won the enemy officer's friendship. A picture exists of the friars with this Lieutenant Zalewski. It was Zalewski, recalls Brother Juventyn, who sought the photo "in token of his friendship." Brother Juventyn's memoirs also recall how, on November 9, the Franciscans were once again herded onto a train, this time headed back to Poland.

> Around 11 o'clock at night, our train stopped in Schildberg (today Ostrzeszow), where armed German soldiers were waiting. We were arranged at once into fives. One of the soldiers noticed Father Kolbe had a cane. Grabbing it, he angrily struck it against Father's chest, growling ``Was ist los? Ein Gefangener mit dem Spazierstock!'' ("What's going on? A prisoner with a cane!") Father Kolbe answered calmly ``Ich bin krank.'' (``I am sick.'')

Shouting "Schnell, schnell!" ("Quickly!"), the soldiers forced the tired, malnourished prisoners to run, beating them with clubs, until they reached their new camp, a converted secondary school the Germans had commandeered from the Salesian Fathers. There the friars slept blanketless on the bare floor. Kolbe was anxious about the health of the near-starving prisoners and thought of a way to get extra food for them. The idea hinged, however, on the goodwill of the German camp commander. A third time, Kolbe succeeded in gaining the affection and respect of an enemy officer. Lieutenant Hans Mulzer, a Protestant Evangelical minister in civilian life, thirty-one years later exchanged letters with Brother Juventyn. Excerpts from two written in December 1970:

> I . . . never will forget the Franciscans in the camp of Ostrzeszow! I tried to ease the stay of the religious in the camp as well as I could under the circumstances. I realized that life there was very difficult. The very imprisonment must have been very depressing. They had to sleep on the floor without blankets. The meals were insufficient, and the forced inactivity was very wearisome. Above all, they felt keenly the lack of spiritual comfort, being deprived of Holy Mass and Holy Communion for weeks. Nevertheless, Father Maximilian Kolbe, with whom I had more contact, as well as his Brothers, never complained to me. On the contrary, they bore their lot with patience and submission. . . .

Precisely what Mulzer did for the prisoners at Kolbe's request, which may well have saved them from starvation, was to purchase some extra food as a supplement to the official ration. He also permitted two prisoners, pushing a hand cart and accompanied by two soldiers, to beg food each day in the town. Anna Lebner, along with her brother Czeslaw, supplied the prisoners with bread and rolls from their bakery. Anna later told Brother Juventyn:

> One day in December 1939, while in the shop, I noticed soldiers leading prisoners. I walked out on the threshold and noticed one Brother walking up to Father Kolbe and whispering something in his ear. Father turned toward me, blessing me with the sign of the cross. I, too, blessed myself. It all happened in a moment. Upon returning into the shop, I burst into tears. That blessing I will never forget as long as I live.

Rumors circulated that the prisoners were soon to be released. Brother Juventyn was among the friars who thought Kolbe, if freed, should immediately go into hiding.

> We urged Father Maximilian to hide himself in some convent of nuns. We warned him against the Germans, who would give him no peace in Niepokalanow. He listened calmly to our recommendations, but gave no immediate reply. Finally, he said to us: "Dear children, I'm grateful for your generous hearts but, unfortunately, I cannot take your advice." God, he felt, wanted otherwise.
>
> One of the Brothers asked him what would happen to the Nazis. He replied, "All this will pass; good must win."

To prepare for the feast of the Immaculate Conception on December 8, the friars began a nine-day retreat under Father Pius Bartosik, who would die this same month just two years later in Auschwitz.

> Father Kolbe gave us a hint on how to benefit from retreats: "Retreat conferences are just aids. The basic aim of a retreat is to penetrate into self and examine one's self as to how we have conformed to God's will—that is, how we have been guided by supernatural obedience."

Brother Jerome had become irritated by Father Maximilian's repeated statements that the friars would be freed and that the Immaculata would be involved. But Kolbe's predictions proved precise. Of the 365 days in the year, only one is the feast recognizing the Immaculate Conception of Mary. On that day, the friars were among three hundred prisoners loaded on a train for Warsaw and freedom. Before they left Ostrzeszow, Brother Juventyn recalls:

> Hans Mulzer, the camp Kommandant, meeting Father Kolbe, handed him 200 grams [about one-half pound] of margarine . . . with a gracious and respectful gesture. . . . Father thanked him kindly and they shook hands in parting.

Mulzer's letters note Kolbe also managed a farewell gift:

> At his departure from Ostrzeszow, Father Kolbe pressed into my hand a medal of the Blessed Virgin Mary, which I cherished as a token of Father's goodwill shown to me. It accompanied me from Poland to Russia and France until August 1944, when the American planes shot at our unit. They hit the car with the officers' luggage, and so everything went up in flames, including my medal.

In a day when ecumenism had not even been whispered of, Mulzer also recalls:

> Father Kolbe invited me to visit his friary whenever an opportunity would arise. He sketched the directions for me on how to find my way to Niepokalanow. . . . I truly intended to accept his invitation. . . .

Brother Juventyn recalls from that trip:

> In Lodz, our train stopped for a while. Some prisoners walked out on the platform. We again proposed to Father Maximilian to seek his safety in flight, for we felt that his stay in Niepokalanow would be threatened. He expressed his gratitude for our concern, but added, "As Guardian, I must be in Niepokalanow, not elsewhere."

The house where Kolbe was born.

Kolbe in Paris boys' choir
(seated, front, far left).

Kolbe as a seminarian in
Rome.

Kolbe (seated sixth from left, first row center) with a group of his first Brothers at Niepokalanow, 1928.

Lumber mill at Niepokalanow, built by Brothers to speed up construction of buildings and keep costs down.

The buildings that comprise Niepokalanow, which Kolbe founded in 1927 near Warsaw, Poland.

Kolbe (center) with the four Brothers who accompanied him to Japan in 1930. On Kolbe's left is Brother Zeno, and on his far right, John Dagis.

Kolbe at his desk in Nagasaki, Japan.

The mission that Kolbe founded in Japan, called the "Garden of the Immaculate," was built on the outskirts of Nagasaki and thus avoided destruction in the atomic bomb explosion in 1945.

Kolbe (upper right) with young candidates for the Franciscan Order.

Kolbe (with beard) after he returned to Niepokalanow from the missions in Japan.

8

Open Heart and Hands

R ELEASED AT 7 A.M., the elated but anxious black-robed friars headed wearily on foot toward Warsaw's Franciscan friary. As they passed Poles whose sagging features and bowed shoulders mirrored the national depression, they skirted the war rubble still being laboriously lifted from the streets by forced labor teams of gentiles and Jews, the latter painfully conspicuous by the white armbands with a blue Star of David that encircled their right arms. The friars tried not to see the erect-postured Germans whose arrogant, uniformed presence seemed to be everywhere and whose military decorum, yesterday's prisoners suspected, barely masked an unholy, self-congratulating glee.

At the friary they learned that arrests of Warsaw priests were continuing in order to cow and terrify the citizenry, who traditionally, in times of enemy occupation, looked to the Church for leadership and spiritual support. Similar persecutions were taking place throughout the country. At the war's outbreak, priests in Poland had numbered 10,217. Over one in three—a total of 3,646— would end up in concentration camps. Two-thirds of those (2,647) would die. (This did not include, of course, the number imprisoned or killed among Brothers and nuns or the Polish Church's lay leadership. Nor did it include the priests, Brothers, nuns, and lay leaders brought from elsewhere in Europe to concentration camps in Poland.)

With this sad news to dishearten them, they took another train south to Niepokalanow. As the black-clad group approached the unimpressive friary entrance, they noticed the empty pedestal where usually the outstretched arms of Mary's statue welcomed her sons. Starting with the statue, which lay broken on the ground, the Franciscans discovered that all the religious symbols which meant so much to them had been desecrated. Going inside, Brother Jerome, who had found Kolbe's optimism about their release so trying, recalls: *continued*

> We found the areas where we produced our publications demolished and the printing machinery partially carried off (the oldest and most primitive pieces alone remained). Father Maximilian was not discouraged by this. With joy he took up new works.

At least, around the shambles, the walls still stood and the humble roof remained intact. And forty Brothers and four priests, who had moved back in during their confreres' nearly three-month imprisonment, were there to welcome them. Among these was Brother Pelagius Poplawski, who had left in the general panic of the war's opening days. Brother Pelagius observed Kolbe's return, as a weak, weary exprisoner, to the plundered friary he had built with such sacrifice:

> I saw that, as he returned from arrest, Father Maximilian was completely serene and self-possessed.

As if still in a state of shock, the forty-four Franciscans had just been living with the mess. Kolbe's arrival drew them out of their torpor. They pitched in as he began at once picking up the scattered files and thrown-about furnishings. The desecrated religious symbols, including the statue of Mary, were repaired and restored to their places.

Most important to all of them, the body of Christ returned to the tabernacle in the humble chapel of rude boards. All day before the tabernacle, friars and priests took turns, in groups of six, adoring their God and begging his grace and protection for the many souls in anguish and trial as 1939 came to its melancholy end.

This concentrated prayer in reparation for the outrages Hitler was perpetrating on humanity was Kolbe's spiritual thrust. He also had to deal with external realities. The source of the friary's humble meals had been its apostolate as Poland's great Christian communications center. Even at Amtitz the irrepressible Kolbe was pondering ways to begin publishing again under the occupation.

For the moment, however, this was impossible. Wasting not a second deploring the shut-down apostolate, Kolbe deployed immediately and brilliantly to feed and protect the flock, a flock that was growing as the friars, now that air raids were no more, trickled back day by day until their numbers reached 349. The Germans had ordered the friary not be home to more than seventy, and seventy were duly registered, but, without sending away a single soul, Kolbe immediately began wearing away at the occupation authorities' resistance to the full complement.

It should not be thought that he struggled to keep his spiritual sons out of some egotistical fear of losing followers. Besides his real concern to help them keep the solemn vows many had made to God, Kolbe also worried lest they fall prey to the Nazis. Able-bodied young men were prime targets for deportation to German forced labor camps (at least 1.3 million Poles suffered this fate), imprisonment in concentration camps, or—particularly as relations with the Russians deteriorated— a simple shot to the head as one less enemy on the German's eastern flank. Brother Pelagius provides insight into Kolbe's brilliant tactics, which saved Niepokalanow and its occupants from enemy hands:

> With the war, the monastic life at Niepokalanow broke down to the point that it seemed completely erased. Father Maximilian, with great trust in God and the intercession of the Immaculate, reorganized with complete success so that [almost] four hundred* of us, Brothers and Fathers, were able to stay together during the entire German Occupation.
>
> He did this by taking up various sorts of work that would (1) utilize every one of us; (2) be of a nature that could not be hindered by the invaders; (3) economically sustain the friary; and (4) benefit the people of the area.

---

*Actual numbers, according to Giorgio Domanski, head of the M. I., are as follows: 1940, 349; 1941, 259; 1942, 307; 1943, 287; 1944, 308.

He organized shops for the repair of farm machines and tools serving the entire region around Warsaw. Over one hundred Brothers worked in these shops alone. And the Germans even provided oil and iron for the work. Father also accepted German orders for us to run a dairy, which benefited the neighborhood as well as satisfying the authorities.

Another Brother adds:

Besides being repaired, farm equipment was also constructed. And we also had other machine shops, bicycle repair, a garage, woodworking and carpentry enterprises, watch repair and clock making, a photographer's shop and lab — even a cheese factory attached to the dairy.

Brother Pelagius again:

With all these undertakings, Father Maximilian not only provided for our material needs but preserved the friary facilities from falling into outside hands while benefiting the entire country.

While setting all this up, having registered the seventy permitted friars, he appealed again and again that Niepokalanow should be legal residence for all the friars, until he [finally] succeeded.

Others recall that one way he succeeded was by showing that every Brother was necessary for the friary's useful occupations, which also included a Red Cross health care center for about fifty invalided soldiers and civilians and work with displaced persons— which alone occupied several Brothers full-time.

While securing the friary spiritually and materially, Kolbe did not forget individuals. Brother Pelagius recalls:

When I found myself in a state of spiritual depression for three months, Father Maximilian was like a mother to me. Unhappy and beaten down in spirit as I was, he sustained my soul, handling me with a mother's tenderness. I owe to him my having come out of it. And I wasn't the only one. I saw and heard that he did the same for all the other suffering confreres. In the conferences he gave the community at this time, he underlined the necessity for us Christians to *hope*.

Brother Lawrence Podwapinski, the community's watchmaker, was also helped by Kolbe's compassion in those dark days:

In February 1940, a period of great poverty for Niepokalanow, I came back from the eastern regions carrying about fifteen watches and a little money that I had earned. At the friary I received word that my elderly mother found herself without anyone to care for her and without any means of support. I asked Father Maximilian if I could send part of the money I had earned to my mother. After okaying it with his Superior, the Father Provincial, Father ordered me to go home to take care of my mother and to take, not part, but all the money. I owe this to his goodness. I also see in it his human and spiritual wisdom because, by doing so, he increased my devotion to the Order and to working for God.

Even in wartime, Kolbe's charity extended beyond Franciscans and their dependents. Back from Warsaw where Kolbe had sent him during the first bombardments because of his bad nerves, Father Florian Koziura noticed "the love and care with which Father Maximilian occupied himself with the needs of the refugees." And it was not just a handful of families or individuals coming to the door for help. Truckloads (Brother Juventyn estimates as many as 1,500 Jews and 2,000 gentiles at one time) were dumped at the friary by the Nazis, displaced persons who had been forced from their homes as "undesirables" in territory annexed by the Reich. The first group (Jews and gentiles from the Poznan area), many times outnumbering the Franciscans, was practically waiting on the doorstep when Kolbe and his malnourished friars returned from imprisonment. As Jesus, out of compassion for a weary, hungry crowd, had fed 5,000 with a few loaves and fishes, Kolbe and the Brothers somehow managed to feed their bedraggled guests until the Germans began alloting food for them. To do so, the friars begged in the neighborhood. Just how a neighborhood in the turmoil of invasion could—or would—feed so many strangers is one of those mysteries that the world wonders at but saints gratefully accept as "the Providence of God." Kolbe not only provided housing (the guests were given about three-fourths of the friary) and food, but clothing and every other kind of assistance as well.

Kolbe himself mentions in a letter the following services to refugees sheltered at Niepokalanow in May 1940: the infirmary was caring for sixty to seventy daily, the pharmacy was dispensing medicine to twenty daily, the little hospital for lay people was housing thirty daily, and the friary kitchen was feeding 1,500. Additionally, furniture was being made for them in the carpentry shop. Even their shoes were being repaired. Brother Pelagius adds:

For the displaced persons he also organized spiritual care — complete pastoral assistance — and he used to visit them [both gentile and Jew, notes Father Florian] to lift their spirits.

Surprisingly, the friary later also gave temporary friendly shelter to 1500 Volksdeutsche (Germans living outside the fatherland) according to the newsletter Kolbe wrote in July 1940 to those friars who had not been able to return to Niepokalanow.

Even after the Germans began allotting rations to the displaced persons from the Poznan area, Kolbe, knowing firsthand the inadequacy of these official amounts, added to them. Father Florian recalls:

Daily he gave twenty kilos of our bread to the displaced persons to supplement what the authorities supplied. At Christmas, too, he ordered a distribution of gifts for the poor children of these families (we had around 3,000 people in the friary at that time).

One of the displaced Poles, Jan Czwojdzinski, years later reminisced to Brother Juventyn about the holiday festivities that were the efforts of Father Maximilian's great heart to build, if only for a moment, sheltering walls of love about these poor victims of hate.

[The holiday] impressed us most profoundly as we experienced during those days so much kindness and concern from the good Fathers and Brothers. We realized that they, too, had just returned from the German camp to their devastated friary, robbed of the most necessary equipment, materials, and supplies. Yet they managed to collect enough surprises for all of us, so that no one felt left out. We were offered baked goodies, and children received little bags of Christmas cookies and candy. In the friars' chapel, a solemn Midnight Mass was celebrated. A soul-stirring jubilation was experienced with mixed emotions, as ardent prayers rose to the merciful Father. . . . Tears rolled down the worried and anxious faces of many. Those moments engraved themselves indelibly in our hearts and minds, evoking everlasting gratitude to the good Franciscan fathers and brothers.

At Father Kolbe's request, a second, non-Christian celebration was put on for the touched and grateful Jewish families on New Year's Day.

Brother Mansuetus Marczewski had noticed that Father Maximilian had an especially tender love for the Jews. This love was reciprocated. Early in the new year (1940), the Poznan deportees were resettled away from the monastery. Before leaving, the Jewish leaders sought out Father Maximilian. According to Brother Juventyn, a spokesperson (Mrs. Zajac) said:

> Tomorrow we leave Niepokalanow. We've been treated here with much loving concern. . . . We've always felt someone close to us was sympathetic with us. For the blessing of this all-around kindness, in the name of all the Jews present here, we want to express our warm and sincere thanks to you, Father Maximilian, and to all the Brothers. But words are inadequate for what our hearts desire to say. . . .

In a loving gesture to Kolbe and his Franciscans, she concluded by asking that a Mass of thanksgiving be celebrated to thank God for his protection of the Jews and the friary. Another Polish Jew added, "If God permits us to live through this war, we will repay Niepokalanow a hundredfold. And, as for the benevolence shown here to the Jewish refugees from Poznan, we shall never forget it. We will praise it everywhere in the foreign press."

Out of his belief that Christ lives, rejoicing or suffering, in every person, Father Maximilian had always helped the many poor who rang the bell in Niepokalanow in prewar days. In the dark days of 1940, in spite of the friary's poverty and a new group of deportees to care for, he continued this policy, trusting in "the bottomless cash box of Divine Providence." Father Florian recalls:

> He gave orders to feed anyone who came to the friary door hungry. It was simply a principle of his to console or help anyone who had problems or sorrows.

Brother Cyprian notes that, if anything,

> [Kolbe] was especially generous with the poor during the Occupation. He also did everything he could for those who were former benefactors of ours, but who were now impoverished due to the war.

Father Vladimir Obidzinski, pastor of the neighborhood church, recalls one concrete form Father Maximilian's concern took:

> For those who died—and they were many—Father Maximilian had coffins made in the friary's woodshops and he gave these free of charge to the poor.

To anxious confreres prone to adding up income and outgo for nervous comparisons, as in the early days of Niepokalanow, Kolbe wryly predicted, "You'll see, we'll come out all right in spite of calculations." Brother Jerome admits:

> I never saw him discouraged even when there were great financial difficulties.

Janina Kowalska, the neighborhood girl at whose home Father Maximilian had stayed in 1917 during the weeks when Niepokalanow was only bare fields, sums up:

> For the poor, Father Maximilian always had an open heart and hands.

9

Kolbe and His Enemies

assisted in the resettlement of displaced personsabout 1500 people (?)

I N FEBRUARY AND March, the Poznan refugees were leaving the friary. In April, 1,500 displaced persons, primarily from Pomerania in western Poland, arrived. This group was at Niepokalanow until July, when some were allowed to return home. Others were ordered to settle in the Warsaw area, an undertaking the Franciscans and their friends assisted with; but some, regarded as more dangerous, were sealed into closed trains and sent out for forced labor to Germany. This group of Poles was never heard from again.

In all, an estimated three million Polish Jews* and three million non-Jewish Poles (one of every six persons in the nation†), including perhaps the entire Gypsy population and one priest in four, would perish between 1939 and 1945. Besides those killed by the Nazis, thousands were slaughtered by the Russians who, on September 17, had invaded from the east. To the Russians go the grisly honors of massacring thousands of Polish army officers and soldiers in Katyn Forest—perhaps as many as 19,000 who "disap-

---

*This left only about 100,000, the prewar Jewish population having been 3,113,900.

†In January 1939, the population was 34.7 million.

peared" during Soviet captivity. Besides those deported by the Germans, several hundred thousand Poles were also deported by Russia to the U.S.S.R., many never to reappear.

It was the Nazis, however, who were in baneful evidence around Warsaw and Niepokalanow throughout the war years, even standing guard at the friary gate. It does not take great imagination to understand how the average inhabitant of the friary, deportee or friar, felt toward the invaders. Only the rarest heart could have found room for the Germans that year in Poland. But at least one heart did. In that mournful period, Maximilian Kolbe cheerfully carried out Christ's command that His followers should love and do good to those who do them evil. The German soldiers at Niepokalanow had desecrated or destroyed statues and saints' pictures in the friary. They had even cut out Poland from the wall maps. Brother Ivo Achtelik remembers how Kolbe repaid them:

> We had a unit of Germans stationed at Niepokalanow to guard a section where they were storing ammunition. One of their noncommissioned officers fell sick and Father Maximilian heard about it from our nursing Brothers. He went right away to visit the sick German, giving him and all his squad medals. The soldiers were deeply impressed by Father's gesture.

Not only did Kolbe not wish on the invaders "what they deserved." Brother Jerome explains:

> The reason Father Maximilian liked to distribute medals to German soldiers whenever possible was not only the hope of bringing them to God, but also of assuring them the intercessory protection of the Virgin Mary.

Needless to say, Germans did not make social calls on the Poles, nor did imprisoned Poles send thank-yous to their captors. Except Father Maximilian. . . . Brother Ivo, who was doorkeeper at that period, recalls a German lieutenant who came more than once to visit Kolbe. As the German left one day he told the Brother, "You have a good and worthy Prior."

Kolbe's thank-you to the mother or mother-in-law of Lieutenant Zalewski, whom he had met at Amtitz:

Dear Madam:
   When I was interned at the camp at Amtitz, I had the good luck to

meet your son. He was the commander of a company there. A group of religious and myself were confided to his care. All of us, dear lady, were struck by his high degree of culture and by his profound sense of justice.

I don't know where he is stationed now, but I want to, through you, dear lady, thank him for everything and let him know that after three weeks stay at the camp in Schildberg, we finally regained our convent. May the Immaculata see that he is rewarded!

Father Maximilian Kolbe

When it comes to loving one's enemies, a Zalewski or an admiring caller is not too tough. But enemies of a more sinister nature also visited Kolbe.

There was, for instance, Ratajczak, the depraved German-appointed administrator of the Polish territory containing Niepokalanow. Very chummy with the Gestapo, he was suspected by some Brothers of having a hand in Kolbe's eventual arrest out of hopes of further plundering the friary. He sent his wagons, in spite of the friars' pleadings, to carry away for his personal use the lumber readied before the war for a church. (Kolbe—forever enamored of Lady Poverty—was still happy with the low frame chapel; but the Brothers, while content with their own lot, dreamed of grander quarters for the tabernacle of their God.) Kolbe said nothing. He may even have been pleased to keep his humble little chapel a while longer. Then, before the wide-eyed Brothers, Ratajczak not only brought his dissolute mistress into the Franciscans' cloister, but into Kolbe's own cell. Gravely but respectfully, because a soul, however besmirched, is of infinite value and must be brought to God at any cost, the Franciscan Superior fearlessly told the Gestapo's chum that he must not break the centuries-old rule that protects the celibate's vow. Ratajczak, deaf to any overtures toward his soul, was not pleased.

Then there was the Gestapo-sent delegation from the Occupation press. These Germans toured Niepokalanow and were treated with the utmost kindness by Father Maximilian, who had a long talk with them on the friary's purely spiritual aims in publishing (he was still applying for permission to put out at least *The Knight*). In response, the Occupation Warsaw daily *Warschauer Zeitung*, edited by the delegation's leader, printed a vicious attack

[handwritten: remained calm & unfettered in the face of the Gestapo's cruelest officers]

on Niepokalanow as a hotbed of activities treasonous to the Third Reich. Kolbe showed no anger but, taking Brother Cyprian with him, traveled by train to Warsaw to protest. In his usual soft-spoken, deliberate tones, Father Maximilian expressed to the editor his sorrow over the paper's defamatory report, which both knew was not only untrue but could be extremely dangerous for the friary. The man listened politely, then coolly blamed the author who, when buzzed, was conveniently "out." (The Brothers believe the article was most likely written on Gestapo orders or at least with Gestapo agreement.) Without even a protest that this article could lead to the imprisonment of every one of his friars, Kolbe returned home.

The Gestapo itself, a group of Brothers writes, "had a special dark interest in Niepokalanow, which was like an irritating speck in their eye." Gestapo men called frequently at the friary, looking for the priest editor of the suspended newspaper (he had fled to the United States with Prince Drucki-Lubecki) or on other sinister errands. Father Florian Koziura says:

> In those grave and unpleasant meetings, Father Maximilian spoke with sober dignity. His behavior toward the Gestapo agents was always completely serene — he had absolutely no fear of them — but prudent.

Brother Ferdinandus Kasz recalls:

> In spite of all of this — the dispersion, imprisonment, numerous oppressions, and deprivations, including even the requisitioning of our food — Father Maximilian not only never showed even anger, let alone hate, for the Germans, but kept exhorting us friars to pray for their conversion and to *love* them.

Brother Juventyn adds:

> He particularly asked the Brothers who knew German to get close to them.

Brilliant tactician that he was, could Kolbe have had the practical motive of making the friary life securer or of living himself "to fight another day"? Apparently not. Brother Ferdinandus Kasz was one of the friars eventually carted off by the Gestapo to Dachau. In Dachau, in 1944 or early 1945, Kasz was collecting written reminiscences on Kolbe so that his dead spiritual father's holiness would not be forgotten. At that time Father Bronislaus Stryczny, one of Kolbe's oldest and closest friends, revealed to his fellow prisoner:

> During the Occupation the Gestapo understood and feared Father Maximilian's uncommon skill at influencing people, a skill that was apparent in his activities even during that period. Because of the possibility of his having an anti-Nazi effect on people through the press, they refused to let him publish. But considering him a valuable and eminent man, the Gestapo was willing to enlist him among their supporters. During the summer of 1940, some of their officials from Sochaczew, by order of the highest governing body in Warsaw, offered German citizenship to him. He would have been registered quite legally under their rules as a "Volksdeutsche," that is, a person of German origins or ancestry. This, of course, was possible because of his Germanic surname. Father Maximilian did not accept this offer, replying that he had always been and wished always to remain Polish. At that, the Germans gave up.

To the friars who would have begged their Father to take this chance to save himself, Kolbe said nothing.

Was he perhaps merely a stubborn Polish patriot? His good friend Sister Felicitas Sulatycka, while in no way denying that Kolbe was a patriot in the wholesome sense of loving his country and being proud of his Polish roots, said he was no narrow nationalist but "often repeated that all the world should live in brotherhood."

If he could not become a Volksdeutsche, this was not out of animosity toward the Germans. To them he might have repeated Christ's words: "If my Father was not permitting all this, you could do nothing." Nor did he suffer from a sense of Polish superiority. He could not align himself in any way with Nazism, neither to save his own life nor—the greater temptation—to secure the lives of the Niepokalanow priests, including the dearly loved Father Pius, and Brothers who also perished at Auschwitz and Dachau. The whole philosophy of Hitler was opposed to everything Christ stood—and died—for.

In resisting this last chance to escape from the Gestapo's enemies list, and surmounting the temptation to save his spiritual family, Kolbe—his conferences of this period make clear—knew that he had set his feet toward his personal Golgotha.

Perhaps it was then that the German spies appeared in the friary "reporting everything." Sister Felicitas says:

Father Maximilian did not complain about these persecutions when he visited our convent, but he asked us to pray for the spies. About two weeks before his arrest, he also confided to me with great sorrow that someone looking for revenge had denounced the Order to the Germans. He said this could have very serious consequences. Then he exhorted me to pray for the soul of the betrayer and *not* for the friary. "I don't care about the friary," he said, "as long as this soul is saved."

10

The Last Months

U NDER THE PRESSURE of the Nazi net gathering about him, the physically frail Kolbe carried his burdens of administrator and Father gracefully. How he did it is a human mystery that can only be solved by understanding the inner life of a saint.

At the point of great sanctity where the individual can truly proclaim, "No longer do I live; but Christ—or the divine—lives in me," there is an overflow of divine energy that makes the physically and emotionally impossible completely possible. Of course, the cares of the apostolate are tediously real and there can be moments of even agonizing fear, such as Christ's in the Garden. Nevertheless, when an individual has thrown everything away for the pearl of great price and becomes one with God, then—like a great silent river hidden under the visible trickle in the sand bed—beneath the real worries and cares of each day, as Kolbe himself said, there is a peace and joy beyond words. Sister Felicitas saw these two streams when, only two weeks before his arrest, he spoke those heroically charitable words about his betrayer. She saw that while Kolbe was suffering real sorrow, at the same time he was as tranquil and serene as ever.

To understand Kolbe, or any saint, it is crucial to grasp this inner stream of joy. Far from that solemn sobriety the ignorant associate with holiness, sanctity is an inextinguishable gladness of heart. The stigmatized St. Francis sang joyously to his divine Love to the end of his life. Kolbe's jokes and smiles in the years 1940 and 1941 are no more feigned than the occasional moments of anxiety he shared with intimates.

And *alter Christus* that he had become—despite the occasional forebodings that were the afflictions of his common humanity and despite the trials of his ministry—he remained joyously confident at his depths that, if God permitted him to suffer and die, He would also triumphantly resurrect him. This gave his sufferings meaning. They were not punishments by a petty or angry God, but the loving Father's "purifying fire" and spiritual coin with which to ransom others. It is this joyous trust that explains the serenity— even the joy—with which he occasionally speaks of his coming martyrdom.

Father Stanley Frejlich, from whom Franciscan joy bubbles even in serious discussion, was, in 1982, the Superior of the Franciscan Province—the largest in the world—in which Niepokalanow is located. Father Stanley came to Niepokalanow in 1934—"thanks be to God," he interjects with a merry laugh—as a junior seminarian. When war broke out he was studying for the Franciscan priesthood at Lwow. He remembers Kolbe in 1940–1941 as his philosophy teacher. This was not normally one of Kolbe's duties, but when the House of Studies at Lwow was closed by the invaders, it was Kolbe who gathered the young men at Niepokalanow where he secretly continued their instructions. (In Cracow at the same time, young Karol Wojtyla was also secretly preparing for the priesthood through the illegal theology department of Jagiellonian University hidden, with several others, in the house of Archbishop Adam Stefan Sapieha during his clandestine study hours.) Father Stanley gives a portrait of Kolbe in his last months of freedom:

> As a teacher he was the best. He shared so much with us from his own life and his own job—especially from his period in Japan. And during our lessons he was wonderfully cheerful—always smiling. And very funny too. He knew lots of jokes and funny anecdotes. One that I remember is a true story of something that happened when he went to a conference of Polish magazine editors before the war. There were some atheistic editors there who believed priests are all stupid and uneducated. I can understand that seeing Father Maximilian, who was al-

ways so humble, so down-to-earth, so simple, they might readily have concluded that here was a prime example. Anyway, Father Maximilian told us that one of these fellows decided to have some fun with the ignorant priest. What he wanted was to expose Father's ignorance before the group. So he penned a note, but not in Polish — in French — and sent it over. He was certain Father would have to say, "I can't read this," to everyone's snickers. Of course, Father Maximilian knew a number of languages — Russian, Italian, German, Latin, and so forth. He got the note. At once he understands what's up. He writes an answer in French but, to have a little fun of his own with this arrogant fellow, midway in the answer he switches to Japanese. The would-be jokester, seeing that he was bested, had the grace to come over to Father and say, "Forgive me, Father. I had no idea you were so clever!"

Naturally we loved this story. I had better add that there was no boasting in Father's telling. He enjoyed the joke and he knew we knew he knew Japanese. He did not ever mention to us all the other languages he had mastered, nor did he ever mention, even though he was teaching us philosophy, that he had a Ph.D. in the subject.

By nature he was very quick and impulsive — what you might call a nervous temperament. For instance, if two of us or two Brothers began arguing, he would immediately say, "Now what's going on here?" But in the next second he would quiet down and say calmly, "My sons, be quiet, please."

Early every morning we went to Mass. Each day after this, Father Maximilian used to walk outside the chapel to and fro, saying his rosary. This was a substitute for the priest's usual obligation to say the Breviary daily [his Superiors had made this modification due to his heavy work load and TB]. What struck me more than anything else about Father Maximilian was how he prayed. In the midst of this bustling spiritual city of three hundred or so, he was so deep in prayer that he saw none of us.

We young students sensed even then that we had with us one who in the future would be a canonized saint. In fact I wrote a testimony — it's in the Niepokalanow archives today — while he was still alive in 1941, for his beatification process — which, of course, was years away. I was that sure that he would eventually be proposed for canonization.

Brother Pelagius recalls Kolbe at this time as an administrator of amazing coolness:

A scene remains vividly in my memory. Father Maximilian was in his office and I was telling him about some business I had taken care of. All

more concerned for others
safety than his own
pred. con ex.

104   A MAN FOR OTHERS

at once the phone rang and simultaneously, through two different doors, came customers for the friary products. With complete calm, Father Maximilian asked the customers if either had urgent business. Both replied, "No." Next he invited them cordially to wait in the outer office a moment, answered the phone and took care of the caller; then, having barely missed a beat, he tranquilly continued listening to my account. The sensitivity and self-possession with which he did all of this remain etched in my mind.

One of the displaced persons in a group leaving Niepokalanow recalls how Kolbe continued to make the friary a sheltering ark from the dark waters of Nazism for as many as possible. Franciszka Kierszka's letter to Brother Juventyn also contains evidence that Father Maximilian had one of the commonest by-products of great sanctity: precognition.

I spoke for the first time to Father Maximilian during the liquidation of the camp. The deportees could settle only on the terrain of the gubernatorial province [around Warsaw]. Having four children and not knowing what to do, I turned to Father Kolbe, telling him I had no means of livelihood since my husband was a war prisoner. Father advised me to stay at Niepokalanow, assuring me that my husband would return, and we would all return happily to our home. He also mentioned that, after my husband's return, we would expect a new arrival in our family, and this prediction was fulfilled.

A woman living in the neighborhood of Niepokalanow has also left her testimony of Father Maximilian in this period. She reports how she came to the friary to ask him, in innocent and deadly anti-Semitism, whether it was "all right" to give handouts to war-impoverished Jews who were begging at her door. Patiently Father Maximilian urged her, she reports, to help the Jews. She quotes the reason he gave: "We must do it because every man is our brother." It is as their loving parent who combined motherly tenderness and fatherly protection that many Brothers recall Kolbe in his last months with them. Brother Cyprian:

He asked me once during this Occupation period how my mother was getting along. When I told him she was living in great poverty, he insisted that I send her a big basket of food.

In 1940 travel was difficult but, notwithstanding the problems in getting there, Father Maximilian used to often go to Otwock to visit one of the Brothers who was laid up there with some chest problem. Father used to say there are three branches of the Christian apostolate: prayer, work, and suffering. Suffering is best because it gives egotism no occasion to grow.

When he came back from any trip, he greeted the confreres with an affection that was remarkable. I know when he greeted me, I was uplifted by his singular cordiality, humility, and simplicity. I noted how he was particularly tender toward the confreres who weren't so strong spiritually. And if he had to correct anyone, he did it in such a way that their dignity wasn't offended. He thought absolutely nothing, however, about his own dignity or the dignity of his office. One day he was talking to a Brother who was thinking about leaving the Order. I was almost scandalized by the humility and self-abasement with which he begged this simple Brother, who was only one among hundreds, to stay.

Brother Jerome recalls:

I remember once during these war days when our Father received a small cake from a woman. He insisted on dividing it into three-hundred-some parts so that each of his sons could receive at least a morsel.

These same sons were sometimes a source of suffering or worry. Father Florian relates:

About this time, three Brothers fled the friary (perhaps thinking they would be safer or hoping to join either the underground or the Polish army in exile; undoubtedly, they did not fully understand that young men picked up by the Nazis at this time tended to end up in a concentration camp or worse). Father was concerned and had us look for them until they were located. Then, with warm kindness and real fatherliness, he persuaded them to stay at Niepokalanow.

Brother Jerome again:

During the Occupation, in one of the buildings of Niepokalanow, was set up a small hospital and clinic for lay people. Our Brothers worked there. I met Father Maximilian once and he told me with great sorrow that a real moral mess reigned there and he was trying to change matters. I know that he was not successful until after his death.

There was also, some Brothers relate, the young friar Gorgonio Rembisz. Rembisz, who had only taken his first (or, as they are called, "simple") vows, was working in one of the machine shops.

There he got the bright idea to make a device that counterfeited grosze, the small coins put into circulation by the invaders. Rather skillful at his work, he was successful. Had this news reached German ears before Father Kolbe's, the entire friary would have been imperiled. As much for his lack of judgment as for his dishonesty, Rembisz had to be expelled.

Fortunately, Kolbe also had the consolation of sons like Brother Lawrence, who says:

> In 1940, in a period of great poverty and hardship for the friary, we received the order from the Occupation authorities that each religious had to peel every day sixty small potatoes [these may have been for the displaced persons; undoubtedly they were not for the friars]. Since the potatoes were very small, the work was fatiguing and disagreeable. Because Father Maximilian had the heavy job of Superior, we volunteered to do his part; but he never let us, and each day he came and peeled with the rest.

Those who knew him well understood that the energy to peel potatoes and carry on his myriad other duties came from his constant inner union with God. More than anything else, young Stanley Frejlich had been struck by the way Father Maximilian became utterly lost in his simple meditation on the rosary. Brother Cyprian says:

> I felt that he loved the Savior above everything else. He often said, "I can do everything in him who strengthens me through his mother."
> This great love of his, seraphic and ardent, showed itself in prayer, in private adoration — if he had a minute free, he always went to the chapel to visit Jesus — and in meditation, which he never skipped even when traveling. For instance, during the fall of 1940 I found myself in his company in the Warsaw central train station. We had to wait five hours for a train. After making meditation at the station, we went over to St. Joseph's chapel in Teresinska Street where he celebrated Mass with great recollection. . . . His love for Jesus also showed in the teachings he gave us Brothers and very much in his conversations.

Brother Arnold Wedrowski, only twenty-one at the time, recalls:

> I was writing from Father Maximilian's dictation in August 1940. We were preparing material for a book on Our Lady. He often told me during this period, "Dear son, you know in Japan heaven was promised

me." I think this promise of Paradise strengthened him so that the many difficulties of his mission couldn't overwhelm him. As to the truth of his words, I had no doubts then and I have none today.

Brother Arnold may be right in thinking that Father Maximilian, in talking about his mystical experience in Japan, was buoying his own spirits. Equally possible is that he was trying to prepare Brother Arnold for those moments—and beyond them—when the distraught young secretary would try to follow his spiritual father into the Gestapo's car.

Brother Cyprian said Father Maximilian's "seraphic and ardent" love of God was visible in his conversation and in the conferences he gave the Brothers. Certainly it was this love that permitted him to look at Poland's tragedy as others could not. In March 1938, before most people thought of a war, he had said to the Brothers:

> During the first three centuries, the Church was persecuted. The blood of martyrs watered the seeds of Christianity. Later, when the persecutions ceased, one of the Fathers of the Church deplored the lukewarmness of Christians. He rejoiced when persecutions returned. In the same way, we must rejoice in what will happen, for in the midst of trials our zeal will become more ardent. Besides, are we not in the hands of the Blessed Virgin? Is it not our most ardently desired ideal to give our lives for her? We live only once. We die only once. Therefore, let it be according to her good pleasure.

Once war came, he did not change his tune:

> "God is cleansing Poland," he said. "After this her [spiritual] light will shine on the world." *

and:

> We are living in a time of intense penance. Let us at least avail ourselves of it. Suffering is a good and sweet thing for him who accepts it wholeheartedly.

---

*Although Poland was a country with much spiritual fervor and many religious vocations before the war, there has been far more zeal and far more vocations after it. Held up to the world as an example of a spiritually vibrant nation and home of the present much-loved pontiff, the image of Poland's light shining on the world does not seem far-fetched today.

How could he see anything so positive in suffering? An excerpt from his writings may cast some light:

> When grace fires our hearts, it stirs up in them a true thirst for suffering . . . to show . . . to what extent we love Our Heavenly Father . . . for it is only through suffering that we learn how to love. . . . In suffering and persecution [we] . . . reach a high degree of sanctity and, at the same time . . . bring our persecutors to God. . . .

In other words, true love wants to give. The greater the love, the more this is so. And the more one gives (suffers) for the beloved, the more love grows. What saves the saint in all this from an unhealthy masochism is his longer view. The suffering, which he does not enjoy for itself but endures willingly as a pledge of his love, will be followed by the rapture of heaven. Kolbe taught his sons:

> God is Love, and as the result must bear a resemblance to its Cause, then anything created lives on love. Not only in pursuing our final End, but also in every action and in every moment of the day, the main motive force should be — Love.

It was certainly love alone that powered Kolbe's tireless efforts to speak again to the Polish people through *The Knight*. Brother Jerome recalls:

> After our return from the [internment] camp, I accompanied Father Maximilian twice to the Sub-Prefect Pott in Sochaczew, who was away each time. Father then talked with other officials in regard to [publishing] *The Knight*.

In December 1939, he wrote Pott a letter in which he said:

> In time we hope to be able to publish in every possible language in the world *The Knight of the Immaculata,* which is motivated only by love. Politics have never entered our goals nor ever will as the enclosed statutes prove.

Brother Jerome recalls that when Father Maximilian left the letter and statutes at Pott's office:

> He stated most emphatically, "For these statutes, I am willing to sacrifice my life at any time." On the first occasion after his return home, he said to us, "Now after our transaction with the German authorities, if

they take us to their camp or take our lives, ours will be a martyr's
death for the faith."

The subprefecture having given little satisfaction, Kolbe next went
to the Board of People's Education and Propaganda in Warsaw.
Brother Cyprian says:

> With his attitude, reasoning, and persuasion he won Dr. Grundmann,
> the director of the Warsaw District board, so completely to his cause
> that on January 20, 1940, the latter called the office of the Governor
> General in Cracow, which responded shortly with a written permit for
> the publication of *The Knight.*
>
> Since the printing machines [the ones that were too old to have been
> appropriated by the invaders] were still sealed with lead, Father Maximil-
> ian and I went to the Gestapo in Warsaw. Upon seeing the permit from
> the Office of Propaganda to print the Franciscans' magazine, one of the
> officers evidenced surprise and walked out of the room with the permit.
> After some time, he returned and told us to come back in two hours for
> the final decision.
>
> When we returned, the officer said, "We will not unseal the ma-
> chines." And when Father asked politely for the return of the permit for
> publication, he was refused.
>
> After leaving the Gestapo quarters, I didn't dare to look Father in the
> eye and we said not a single word. I felt especially guilty, since I had
> suggested the idea of approaching the Gestapo. But Father did not re-
> proach me. To keep me at peace, he didn't even mention the subject.
> In fact, he even tried to cheer me up. This incident certainly proved to
> me how deeply spiritual our Father was. He did not stop, however, in
> his efforts to resume [publishing] *The Knight.*

The Third Reich was not stupid. It knew a dangerous man
when it saw one. And Kolbe knew it knew. But even after his
audacious refusal that summer to register as a Volksdeutsche, he
doggedly persisted in his publication applications. All efforts failed
until two and a half weeks before the feast of the Immaculate Conception, a day that always seemed associated with special graces for
Mary's knight. A letter from the Warsaw board announced permission to print one issue only of *The Knight.*

Father Isidore Kozbial was editor. He remembers:

> Father Maximilian told me while I was preparing the single issue we

were to put out during the Occupation, "It isn't important whether *The Knight* gets out, but it is important that the endeavor be surrounded by prayers. Each issue must be prepared 'on our knees' — that is, with prayer — and be sent out accompanied by prayers."

Kolbe wrote one article, not the lead but the last. Titled simply "The Truth," it said:

No one can alter truth. What we can do and should do is to search for truth and then serve it when we have found it.

Somehow they managed to produce the magazine in two and a half weeks so it could appear on Our Lady's feast day, December 8, 1940. Studies for the priesthood and Brotherhood had gone on secretly during the past year. Now, on the same day, having completed their spiritual formation and training under the noses of the Germans, including the friary spies, twenty-two men courageously made vows to live for God as Franciscan friars to Father Kolbe. As though these were normal times, they even posed for a group photo. Most look sober. Three or four dare to smile. Kolbe simply looks tired. Was he pondering that the next souls he formed would be in Auschwitz? Certainly he had no illusions that a Reich built on lies would take kindly to *The Knight's* words on truth. Brother Juventyn recalls father Maximilian's wary handling of the run of 120,000 copies:

As mailing *The Knight* through the post office was rather risky [the Gestapo could simply have confiscated the periodical], the greater part of the edition was delived by personal means starting December 8 in Warsaw, where the inhabitants and the clergy accepted *The Knight* with great enthusiasm. Reappearance of the periodical seemed a sign of the early resurrection of Poland.

In fact, according to a group of Niepokalanow friars:

This issue published during the Occupation produced an incredible enthusiasm among the Poles. Great numbers of letters poured into Niepokalanow from its readers. There were even letters with patriotic slogans like, "The Dawn of Liberty Arises." . . .

Such letters were dangerous for the friary, but—ever the optimist—Kolbe began applying to publish more issues. Brother Juventyn remembers that he had even dated the single issue December/January, trying to pave the way for at least bimonthly publication. Copy was in preparation. At the same time, the friars remember:

During the year [1940] he had given conferences to us in which he led us to understand he would not be at Niepokalanow much longer. As January 1941 opened, he repeated "I shall not live through this war." From Polish people he trusted, who were working (in secretarial positions) at the Gestapo, he was warned by an ersatz business letter that the Gestapo were going to arrest him. Still Father remained at Niepokalanow.

In [1941] German terror in Poland reached its apex. The Germans knew that in a very short time they would be at war with Russia and were afraid, so they were trying to guarantee their flank by massacring as many people as possible in Poland, especially the important people.
. . . Governor General Frank encouraged his men by saying, "We must exterminate the Poles rapidly and efficiently the way we handled the professors of the University of Cracow."*

Mass arrests began. In Warsaw, every day, the prisons bulged. Yet every day hour after hour loaded cars left them for Palmiry where the prisoners were shot.
. . . Hundreds of priests, diocesan, or members of the religious orders, as well as lay Brothers, were shot by the Nazis, who imprisoned some thousands in prisons or concentration camps.

Asking the Germans why they were "destroying the Polish clergy" with these wholesale arrests, the Polish Bishops were answered, "Because in Poland, Church and Nation are one. . . ."

Special revenge of the cruelest kind was reserved for influential people who before the war were known to the Nazis as opponents of Hitler's movement, its activities against the Church, and its policies of conquest. With quick and deadly skill, the Gestapo picked up these people and liquidated them. There was not even formal arrest many times. Individuals simply disappeared.

In Kolbe's case, he was not only a priest and leader of the Franciscans, but an opinion-molder and member of the Polish intelligentsia as the leader and the spirit behind the greatest publishing

---

*Summoned to a meeting, they were arrested en masse and sent to Orianberg concentration camp.

center in Poland. Just as they cried out against the anti-Church policies of Communist Russia, Niepokalanow's publications had deplored Hitler's anti-Church and conquest policies. The Nazis ignored the fact that Kolbe himself had never written on anything but spiritual matters, leaving politics in his publications to lay people. The fact that he was not pro-Hitler and had remarkable power to influence others was more than enough in 1941. The Gestapo called at the friary. They ordered, and were given, a list of all ex-friars. Apparently Kolbe would not disappear. Instead, the Nazis would find someone willing to lie, and would build against Kolbe a neat and completely false case.

While the Gestapo interviewed frightened ex-Franciscans, Kolbe carried on. To those who clamored nervously, "What will happen to Niepokalanow if you're arrested? What will become of us?" he said reassuringly, "It will be nothing—only the changing of the guard."

11

Arrest

I T IS GOOD," Kolbe once said, "to wear oneself out working for God and go to him still young." True to such ideas, he would work until the moment of his arrest. *In January*
On January 4 and again on January 9, he petitioned the highest Board of People's Education and Propaganda in Cracow for permission to publish a February *Knight* and a 1941 calendar. Brother Pelagius recalls:

> He told me openly about this time — mid-January — that the Gestapo would be coming for him. I noticed that he didn't seem afraid, but he intensified his efforts to spiritually prepare the entire friary for the possibility of persecution.

As part of this preparation, he gave a few Brothers a conference on the relationship of the Trinity to Mary the Mother of God. Brother Rufinus remembers:

> Later that same day he asked me, "My son, did you understand what I said?" "No," I answered. Then Father knelt and asked me to kneel with him. He bent his head until it touched the ground and I copied him. Then he prayed and I prayed with him. In this concrete way, he wanted

113

to show me that prayer is necessary to understand the revelations of faith.

On January 24, he managed one of his typically brief letters to his mother:

> Dearest Mother,
> We are trying to get a permit for the February edition of *The Knight.* However, may the Immaculate Mother herself guide our work. Prayer is essential. With a filial embrace and asking your prayers . . .

Six days later, his printing petitions were rejected with the accompanying command to submit no more "requests for printing until further notice."

Perhaps the Gestapo did not have much luck finding ex-friars with malice toward Father Maximilian; perhaps they simply preferred to design their own accusations. In any case, they got their signed statement of Kolbe's treasonous activity by stealth. Gorgonio Rembisz gave the following testimony to the Niepokalanow Brothers in 1941, after Kolbe's arrest:*

> After my expulsion from the Order in January 1941 (which was my own fault, for what I did in my lack of prudence could have endangered the entire friary), I didn't go home right away but stayed in Warsaw. After a few months I went back to my hometown of Rzeszow to the Sisters of Charity where I had had my schooling. Sister told me that the local Gestapo were collecting information on me and wanted to see me as soon as possible. Being afraid of deportation to a German concentration camp, I didn't go. I didn't even register with the authorities for a residence permit. But in two weeks I was called again and this time there were threats. I still didn't want to go, but pushed by Sister Superior and knowing my refusal could imperil the convent, I went. The Gestapo asked through an interpreter if Father Maximilian was involved in politics. They ordered me to repeat Father's words to a certain German. . . . I answered that I didn't know this German—Lempke was his name— and I had no knowledge whether Father Maximilian was involved in

---

*Years later in the Beatification hearings, Rembisz gave a longer, more detailed testimony of his grilling by the Gestapo, which actually took place not once but on two further occasions.

politics. I told them I had never heard him say anything negative about the Germans. He must have been informed on politics since a daily paper had been published in Niepokalanow, but all the political articles were written by laymen. Following this interrogation, I was given a summary transcript to sign which was written in German. I do not know German, but suspecting nothing, I signed.

Rembisz's deposition, which had no relationship to the interview he actually took part in, would later be shown to a number of people who tried to secure Father Maximilian's release as proof that the priest was too dangerous, his activities against the Reich too nefarious, to permit his remaining free. In the sense that love is always dangerous to evil, they were undoubtedly right. From somewhere—perhaps his secretary friend at the Warsaw Gestapo—Kolbe learned that he had been betrayed (whoever saw the document had no way of knowing Rembisz hadn't known what he signed) by one of his own. Sorrowfully, he prayed—not for himself, but for the betrayer—and asked Sister Felicitas to do the same. So as not to upset the Brothers, he said nothing to them. In spite of this precaution, those at the friary were worried. The young seminarian Stanley Frejlich, who today is Father Provincial to the Warsaw Province, recalls:

> I was upset. February 1941 was such a frightful time and we knew that the Germans were going to do something bad to Father Kolbe. I went to his room—it was just a few days before his arrest. He didn't deny it. He said yes, he would be imprisoned by the Nazis, who hated him very much. The Gestapo would come and take him away. He embraced me and said, ``My child, you must love the Blessed Virgin Mary and tell everyone about her.''

Brother Marcellus Pisarek remembers the day before Kolbe's arrest:

> That evening [February 16], during our recreation period, I had the joy of being with him in a small group off to one side from the main group. We were talking primarily of spiritual matters and someone said that God accomplishes the desires of souls who sincerely love him. Then I asked Father Maximilian if this was truly possible. He answered it was, and began giving examples from the lives of the saints, particularly Thérèse of the Child Jesus. He continued, ``God can do everything and

gladly gives himself to the one who has completely consecrated his soul to him." Then Father explained that between God and such a person's soul, a movement of love is continuously passing back and forth. "What indescribable happiness!" he exclaimed and added (rather inappropriately to the discussion), "What a great grace it is to be able to seal with our own life our ideals." Those were his last words to me on the eve of his arrest.

Later that evening, he asked five brothers, including Brother Gabriel and several others who had been with him from the earliest days at Grodno, to join him for a little conference. He had a small cake, Brother Gabriel recalls, which they shared. They all felt it was a very special, somewhat solemn occasion. Kolbe spoke to them on the relationship of Mary, the Mother of God, to the Holy Trinity. In spite of the complexity of the topic, Brother Gabriel recalls:

> Father Maximilian spoke so nobly and so accessibly that we understood very well. Later, however, when one of the participants tried to write down this explanation of the Immaculate Conception, he found it impossible. Then he understood the words of Father Maximilian that "only by asking on one's knees" — that is, by the grace of God — "can one understand such profound mysteries."

As pleased as the Brothers were by Kolbe's special gesture to them, not one realized—until later—that it was his way of thanking them for their friendship and saying goodbye.

Brother Pelagius recalls something else unusual Kolbe did that night, as if he knew these were his final hours with his sons:

> It must have been between the hours of midnight and two in the morning when he telephoned and awakened me. He came to my cell. Reopening the spiritual conversation that we had during the day, he urged me to fidelity toward the Lord and devotion toward the Immaculate. After a while he shared with me the following prayer, begging me to repeat with him, "Immaculate Conception, Immaculate Conception, Immaculate One of God, Immaculate One of God, my Immaculata, my Immaculata, our Immaculata, our Immaculata." A little later, he made his way back to his quarters.

In this seemingly childish prayer chant (which Kolbe scholar Giorgio Domanski points out profoundly sums up Kolbe's ideals),

Father Maximilian reveals again his likeness to the greatest mystics. In the landmark study *Mysticism*, Evelyn Underhill explains that at the height of sanctity, while carrying on the most successful and complex life as apostle, administrator, or evangelizer, interiorly the saint has become the child who alone can fully possess, as Jesus said, the kingdom of heaven. David, the great Jewish mystic, danced for joy before the ark. Picking up her heavy brown skirts, Carmelite Teresa of Avila danced in prayer well past middle age and used to croon "nonsensical little ditties" to Jesus while she swept the cloister. Catherine of Genoa babbled little prayers similar to Kolbe's.

In a conversation at Niepokalanow, Brother Rufinus, another close friend of Kolbe and his personal secretary during this period, told interviewer Diana Dewars of another unusual occurrence that morning. At about 4 A.M., an hour before the usual rising time, Kolbe awoke Brother Rufinus. As they spoke, Kolbe's expression was sober and at one point he had tears in his eyes. Brother Rufinus wondered that Kolbe was wearing his good habit—the unpatched one usually reserved for feast or holy days—but he didn't ask the reason. In retrospect, he too realized Kolbe had been saying goodbye.

That morning, a call from Warsaw warned that a deputation "from the authorities" would be coming. Leaving word with Brother Ivo, the doorkeeper, to call him as soon as they arrived, Kolbe went on dictating his book to Brother Arnold Wedrowski, his secretary in business matters. Brother Arnold recalls that as they worked, at one point, Kolbe suddenly knelt and prayed the "Glory Be," Catholicism's traditional prayer in praise of the Trinity, and the "Hail Mary," which asks the Mother of God's intercession.

At a quarter to ten the telephone rang. Father Maximilian answered. It was Brother Ivo, announcing that three black cars had just pulled in. Both Brother Ivo and Brother Arnold noticed that Kolbe seemed startled or shaken for a second. "Already," he murmured. Then, immediately, his self-possession returned and he said, "Good, good, my son." He went outside the building to greet the Gestapo with the words, "Praised be Jesus Christ."

"Are you Kolbe?" responded the leader of the four uniformed SS men. He alone wore civilian clothes and the ubiquitous Gestapo

was expecting. prepared for
the Gestapo; was kind toward
them

118   A MAN FOR OTHERS

overcoat. Standing in the courtyard, they began interrogating the priest on the things he was teaching his young Franciscans. (Seminaries were forbidden.) Kolbe countered politely that the Franciscans had no students that they hadn't had before the German take-over. Then, refusing to see in any man an enemy, he invited them to see the friary workshops. Perhaps forced by his goodness to assume a more human stance, they actually accepted and several Brothers, blocking a path as they moved some wood, recall how Father Maximilian said calmly to them, "Let these gentlemen by, please, my sons." From his manner they thought he was simply escorting friary guests. After the tour, they returned to Kolbe's office.

There the official arrest was made. Kolbe and five of the friary's six priests were cited. Fathers Justin Nazim, Urban Cieslak, and Anthony Bajewski were summoned from their day's duties. Also called was Kolbe's dear friend Father Pius Bartosik, who had already endured imprisonment with him at Amtitz. It was he whom Kolbe had hoped would one day succeed him as Superior of Niepokalanow. The fifth priest cited with Kolbe, the nervous Father Florian Koziura, escaped arrest because all swore in good faith that he had gone to Warsaw; actually, he had changed his mind and, knowing nothing, was in his room.

As the group of black-robed Franciscans and their captors started for the black cars that had carried so many to torture, imprisonment, or death, Stanley Frejlich was watching sadly with the other seminarians from their classroom window, while a number of Kolbe's sons trailed after their Father. Brother Lawrence recalls how Kolbe's behavior was full of dignity and calm as he formally turned his authority as Superior over to one of the priests not on the Gestapo list. Someone handed him a coat. Brother Rufinus remembers Kolbe comforting him with the words, "The Virgin Mary will take care of you." Brother Pelagius says:

> I observed him every moment following behind as he was led from the friary toward the Gestapo car. I took advantage of a momentary chance to hand him a bag holding some buttered bread. He was sober but calm.

And Brother Arnold:

> My only thought was to go with him. But when I tried to follow

Father Maximilian into the car, the Gestapo men prevented me. They said I was too young and that Father would be coming back soon. I looked at his recollected face and I could read in his eyes the sadness and the love for Niepokalanow and for all of us who were there.

As the cars pulled away, Brother Pelagius says:

> I saw how, just before leaving our sight, he saluted us with a nod of his head, as we stood on the drive.

Maximilian Kolbe would never see Niepokalanow or his spiritual sons again. With heroic trust that God would sustain them, he left them sadly but calmly. They, however, felt no calm. Although they still had a Superior, Father George Wierdak, who had been in charge of the students for the priesthood, at that moment the Brothers standing before the friary felt they were a flock without their good shepherd, surrounded by ravenous wolves. For many of them, too, the dreaded black cars would call. Some would follow Kolbe home to God in martyrdom. A surprisingly large number, however, would survive even death camps to carry on his ideals of love of God, devotion to the Immaculate Mother of God, and service to humanity.

For the moment, acutely depressed, they huddled together in grief, then moved silently, numbly, toward the chapel.

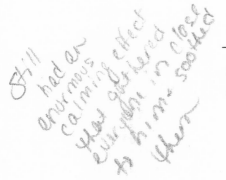

12

Pawiak Prison

THE BLACK CARS snaked through the gray winter's day to Warsaw's Pawiak Prison. A former Polish institution, Pawiak had been taken over by the Gestapo as a sort of holding pen for those being interrogated or whose disposition was otherwise pending. Once in its claws, many left for the "shooting gallery" at Palmiry, others for concentration camps. Few ever simply went home. At the war's end, before the German retreat from Warsaw, the Gestapo shot as many of the last prisoners as was feasible, evacuated the rest for finishing off elsewhere, and then blew up the place. Its ruins remain as a monument with a plaque to those who suffered and died there.

Father Justin, one of two out of the five Franciscan priests to survive their imprisonment, recalled how, in his depression over being arrested, it was the older, frailer Kolbe who cheered him up. "His words," said Father Justin, "gave me great consolation."

Kolbe was also a consolation to others in the large cell where the priests were first placed. Thaddeus L. Chroscicki, later an engineer in the field of wood technology, recalls:

All of us prisoners in the cell—we numbered about thirty—had in

120

Father Maximilian the best of spiritual protectors and fathers. His whole person exuded something so calm and soothing that we all clustered close to him.

Although I was rather young, I liked to listen as he and the others spoke about politics and social and religious questions. By asking questions and leading discussions and conversations, he created a more relaxed atmosphere, helped us forget [our fear and anxiety], and saved us from pessimism and despair. [Yet when our troubles were spoken of], whatever our pains, he understood what we were going through and helped us with advice, comfort, and encouragement. He was really our bulwark against spiritual dejection and encouraged us to be strong and to persevere.

If our cell was a quiet one, this was undoubtedly due to his influence. Even prisoners who were inclined to be skeptical about people, after being with him, soon spoke their approval and respect for him. If conflict between prisoners did occur, he knew how to intervene with great tact and restore calm. I was young, as I said — only twenty-two — and did not know how to give proper value to everything, but I believe his conduct among us grew out of his love for God and his role as one who somehow bore God within him.

When I saw him praying, I could see his profound union with God. And when he was persecuted because he wore his Franciscan robe, something he could have avoided by taking it off (which we advised him to do), he for a long time refused to do it, feeling that he should be distinguishable by his clothing and if this brought him ill treatment he should suffer it gladly for God's sake.

I recall too that when it was suggested that he occupy some relatively more comfortable position in the cell, he always refused.

In all this he never tried to make himself superior to others — I would rather have to describe him as a simple man who looked for places where he could be of help. He might well have considered me not much and paid little attention to me, but in fact he took an interest in me and gave me his sympathy and protection. And this continued later on as much as possible (it was hard to get together there since we were not in the same barracks) in Auschwitz, where I never met him without coming away relieved in soul and stronger in my will to resist.

On February 21, the Franciscans were permitted to send their first card to Niepokalanow. All mail was strictly rationed, just as it was in the concentration camps. Once or twice a month (varying from period to period), a standard card could be written in German. New prisoners must use the small space to explain regulations on incoming mail or to request necessities. Others were required to state precisely what letters and food or other packages had been received. There could be no complaints or even accounts of illness. If a prisoner could not write German, the individual had a choice: He could pay a few precious cigarettes or vital foodstuffs to someone else to write, or he could do without. Incoming mail was also strictly censored. In Father Kolbe's handwriting:

> Send to each of us a wool shirt, a pair of underwear, two pairs of socks, 2 towels, 2 handkerchiefs, a toothbrush, and toothpaste. Send the packages separately. Write the sender's name on it. Send us by mail 10 zlotys [a very small sum, perhaps intended for stamps].

Meanwhile the Franciscan Provincial Superior was tediously pursuing the labyrinth of official channels trying to get the group released. Twenty Niepokalanow Brothers took a more direct route. They wrote, signed, and sent the following message straight to the Gestapo:

> We, the undersigned, address this request to the Commander of the Security Police, politely begging that we may be imprisoned in place of our Fathers. We declare that no one is ordering or obliging us in any way to do so. We take this grave step of our own free will. We are ready to gladly bear ourselves all the accusations [against them] and all the consequences that might follow.

Among the signatures are those of Brother Ivo, Brother Arnold, Brother Jerome, Brother Rufinus—even Brother Dionigi, whom Kolbe had scolded for stealing the bucket of soup in Amtitz. Kolbe probably never knew that his sons volunteered, if necessary, to die for him. But his next postcard can still be read as an unwitting reply to their worry over him and the others:

March 13

All the Brothers must pray very much and well. Work with fervor and don't worry too much about us because nothing can happen to us without the permission of God and the Immaculata.

The priests from Niepokalanow were soon separated. Jan Szegidewicz remembers having Kolbe as a cellmate for a while. During this time, Szegidewicz, who is of Tartar descent, was taken out for questioning and badly beaten. When he was shoved back into the cell, Father Maximilian was all tenderness and tried to console him by speaking about Jesus. Szegidewicz moaned that he was a Moslem, and recalls:

> He showed great delicacy of feeling at this. He took no advantage of the occasion to try to force his religious beliefs on me. He showed real insight, I thought, and distracted me with questions about Moslem religious customs, our holy days, and about other Tartars in Poland. He did his best to create a positive atmosphere in which one could be optimistic and believe in survival.
>
> One day two prisoners who had been at Auschwitz were put in the cell. Father Kolbe asked about conditions there, but neither he nor I could believe what we heard. It seemed such things could not be true.

Edward Gniadek was arrested by the Gestapo on January 12, 1941. In March, after having been kept only in solitary confinement, he was put in a cell with a Jewish Pole he recalls only as Singer. He says:

> After a few days Father Maximilian Kolbe was added to our cell. He was wearing a Franciscan habit and was clean-shaven. The presence of Father Kolbe, who differed so greatly from us by his calm, the things he told us, and conversation with him, calmed me and had the best possible effect on my nerves, which were very bad since each day I lived under the anxiety of being interrogated again—I had not only been beaten but had witnessed the torture of others—or of being sent to a concentration camp.
>
> About the second or third day after Father Kolbe joined us, one of the Gestapo men looked into our cell. He rushed in, somehow infuriated by the sight of Kolbe in his habit, from which hung the usual Franciscan rosary with its crucifix. I saw everything, but it was Singer afterwards who gave me the exact words, for I know no German.
>
> The Scharführer*—that was his rank—grabbed the rosary and, jerking on it, began haranguing Father Kolbe, who made no reply. Then the man pointed scornfully to the crucifix and snarled, "Do you believe in that?"

---

* Platoon leader.

"Yes, I believe," Father Kolbe answered him serenely.

Aroused to a fever pitch, the assailant slapped the priest hard in the face. He grabbed the crucifix, again demanding, "You really believe, eh?"

"Yes, I believe," Father Kolbe again answered calmly.

With each affirmation, the SS man became angrier and more violent (I don't know — maybe it was the priest's calm and determination). Anyway, after each reply he struck Father Kolbe in the face again and again.

But finally, seeing that Father Kolbe could not be shaken, he gave up and stomped angrily from the cell, slamming the door.

I must say again that, during everything, Father Kolbe showed not the slightest agitation. After the Scharführer left, he simply began walking to and fro in the cell, praying silently. On his face were the red marks of the blows. My nerves were very shaken by what had happened and I said something — I can't remember what. He turned to me and said, "Please, I beg you, don't be upset; you have a lot of worries and troubles of your own. What happened just now is really nothing because it's all for my little mother (he meant the Mother of God)." The way he said this you would actually have thought nothing at all had happened.

That same day one of the lower ranking guards who was Polish came in with a prisoner's uniform, recommending that Father Kolbe put it on. He said that if Father Maximilian had been wearing the uniform he would never have been beaten. Lots of prisoners wore their own clothes, but the religious habit drove the Nazis into a frenzy and provoked such incidents.

The other Niepokalanow priests were sent to Auschwitz about the first of April. Kolbe remained in Pawiak. There are no witnesses to his interrogations, but he ended up in the prison hospital with pneumonia. Cleverly, he sent his allowed postcard with no message—only the date, April 2, and the heading "Warsaw, Penitentiary Infirmary." That got by the censor. After a stay there—so much stranger is life than fiction—in this citadel of torture and death, he ended up working in the prison library (undoubtedly a feature of Pawiak not added by the Gestapo, but left over from past Polish administrations). Another priest-prisoner remembers they heard each others' confessions among the books. He also recalls Kolbe as having had a remarkable influence on the young members of the Polish intelligentsia when such prisoners were allowed access to the library.

On May 1, Kolbe was permitted another postcard. To his sons he wrote:

> I have received the packages for Easter. I have also received the cards from Brs. Felice, Ivo, and Arnold. Our loving mother, the Immaculata, has always looked out for and will continue her maternal care for her sons. I stayed some time in the infirmary and am still receiving infirmary rations. At present I am working in the prison library. Today begins the beautiful month of May, the month consecrated to the Madonna. I hope you will not forget me in your prayers. I wish all the Brothers the blessings of the Immaculata and salute all warmly.

His last card is dated May 12, about two weeks before his transfer to Auschwitz:

> My dearest ones
>
> Please send me a civilian suit. I write this by order of the Commander. I don't need shoes because those I have are still in good condition. In place of shoes, please send a work jacket, a vest and a wool scarf. As soon as possible! I received the food parcel on the fifth and the letters of Brothers Pelagius and Felicissimus. For all this I thank the Immaculata. I cannot reply separately to each one because writing is restricted. But I [must] indicate each thing received in each card. Let us promise to let ourselves be led more and more completely how and where the Mother of God wishes so that fulfilling our duty to the utmost, we may through love, save all souls.

13

Auschwitz

T O *SAVE ALL SOULS.* In the death camp, Maximilian Kolbe would tell his friend John Lipski, "No one's conversion is impossible," and urge prayer for the Nazis. The enormity of that heroic charity and unquenchable faith in the goodness and power of God and possibilities for change in every man can only be appreciated by those who grasp in a small way (to know much more is not good for mental health, unless one is a saint) what Auschwitz was.

Auschwitz is the German name for the Polish town of Oswiecim. It is perhaps just that the site of such crimes should still be known by the name its perpetrators gave it rather than its innocent Polish title. The site was carefully selected by the SS in 1940 for several reasons. First, the surrounding area had few inhabitants. Those farmers and villagers who had the misfortune to live in the swampy, unhealthy meadows near the small Polish town lying in the fork of the Vistula and Sola rivers were given orders to leave, and an area of forty square kilometers (fifteen square miles) surrounding the camp was zoned off. Here signs warned, "Forbidden area! Trespassers will be shot without warning!" Observation towers punctuated that warning, as did armed patrols. Within this sector, besides Auschwitz, a number of satellite camps and one huge sister camp called Birkenau were eventually built.

Although the swampy meadowlands were damp and muddy and the air was unhealthy, the SS men were well-fed and precautions were taken to ensure their health. Regulations forbade SS families from using unboiled water for drinking or washing dishes. This was in order to protect them from typhoid, malaria, and other diseases. (For the prisoners, no such precautions were taken. If disease exterminated a few prisoners before they could be shot or otherwise killed, so much the better.)

Besides its lonely location, the Nazis also liked the fact that this fork of two of Poland's rivers was at the center of Nazi-occupied Europe. This made transporting the camps' victims more convenient.

A group of old, abandoned Austrian military barracks still stood from the days when this portion of Poland had been under the Hapsburgs. These fourteen single-story and six two-story buildings were the innocent nuclei around which Auschwitz, and later Birkenau and the smaller satellite camps, would form and spread like ugly cancers on the countryside. This primary camp was at once made secure from escape with concrete posts supporting a double barbed-wire fence through which passed a 220-volt, three-phase current. Where the Sola meandered near, a three-meter (almost ten-feet) high concrete wall strung with the live wires cut off even a view of the river. On the inner side of the entire fence a wide graveled zone made a death belt, within which any prisoner would risk being shot.

SS men ran the camp. Under them, hard-core German criminals serving long sentences in civil prisons were brought in and given authority over the prisoners. They were promised they would eventually be allowed to join the German army if they did a good job on the enemies of the Third Reich. Known as capos, many of these men, according to camp survivors, were the worst kind of perverted sadists. They seemed to vie to see who could kill the most or use the vilest methods. There were thirty of them, and they received prisoner numbers 1 through 30.

The first transport of prisoners, 728 Poles, arrived on June 14, 1940. They became numbers 31 through 758. They were at once put to work enlarging and building new facilities.

Nineteen-year-old Jan Dudzinski and two pals were walking down a back country road after the fall of Poland, on their way out of the country to join the Polish army in exile. The Gestapo picked them up and sent them to Auschwitz where only Jan survived. Ironically, they were fingered by Polish Jews forced to serve in the Nazi Militia to buy a little time for themselves and their loved ones. By such tortuous methods, the invaders tried in every country to pit gentile and Jew against each other. If there was anti-Semitism for them to build on, as there was in Poland, so much the better. Jan, prisoner number 3514, nineteen years old at the time, remembers:

> If there was nothing else to do, they kept us busy digging holes and then filling them. But before long that stopped as the camp became more organized and jobs were assigned. Neighboring farmers had been forced out, leaving their crops still growing. We took in the harvest — for the Gestapo's table. Once walking to work, I saw a little hole in front of me. I decided to jump over it, just to see how strong I was. I fell to the ground in a heap. Luckily, I was able to get up and keep going.

Why would a young man of nineteen be that weak? This is the camp diet on which men and boys did heavy forced labor: Breakfast: half a liter of "coffee" made from acorns, grains, or herbs. The main meal: about three-fourths liter of watery soup and bread,* one loaf to four men, with perhaps the addition, depending on the day, of an ounce of margarine or cheese or a tablespoon of preserves or half an ounce of sausage. Francis Mleczko, a survivor, recalls sausage only on Adolf Hitler's birthday! The official camp diet sheet called for 2,150 calories for those engaged in heavy labor and 1,738 calories for those engaged in medium labor, according to Polish writer Adolf Gawalewicz. (Actual calory requirements for a man doing hard labor are 4,800, with medium labor requiring 3,600.) In *fact,* those in heavy labor got closer to 1,700 calories and the rest about 1,300, says Gawalewicz, although it is impossible to determine precisely the food or calory intake of prisoners because of the many variables. For example, calories were lost when

---

*This bread, survivors say, was dark, heavy, wheatless food like nothing they had ever seen outside the camp. Corn was the only one of its ingredients they could positively identify.

guards stole ingredients for the soup or the bread supplements from the kitchen. Further, the ration of a prisoner might be stolen by criminals among the prisoners who preyed on the weak. Finally, for "disciplinary purposes," rations could be halved. Father Conrad Szweda, a close friend of Kolbe's among the prisoners, recalls a day when many Polish priests were called out of various barracks and put in one group with their bare rations halved. By this and worse means, this particular group was soon done away with. In general, survivors agree that there were more deaths from starvation in this early period, when Kolbe was there, than in later years.

After the German defeat, SS Kommandant of Auschwitz Rudolf Höss testified that besides the millions executed in Auschwitz, the satellites, and Birkenau, 500,000 starved to death. There were so many deaths of this kind that a word was coined for someone suffering advanced starvation symptoms. He was called "a Mussulman."

The first mass execution—the shooting of forty Polish men— took place on November 22, 1940. With their faces to this same wall, thousands would be killed—usually a group each Monday— over the next four years by a shot in the back of the neck. What was the Reich trying to gain by starving and executing Poles who, for the most part, had taken part in no political activities against anyone? As previously mentioned, the Germans feared enemies on their flank who might hinder their planned invasion of Hitler's erstwhile ally, the Soviet Union. To prepare for this event, the first months of 1941 were a time of mass shootings and imprisonment of Polish males. By June, Hitler felt safe invading Stalin's territory.

The Reich's policies were served by death camps in five other ways, according to Gawalewicz. By its very existence, a camp like Auschwitz caused horror and panic in millions who feared they might end up there for the simplest activity. Thus Auschwitz and the other concentration camps were coldly calculated instruments of terror meant to break the will to resist of the overwhelmed nations of Europe. Beyond terrorizing people, Auschwitz was an extermination center for specified groups of society and certain peoples and nations, including the Poles.

Along with other camps, it was also a center of slave labor. This aspect became increasingly important as Germany's own manpower became more and more depleted and inadequate to the war effort. When Kolbe was imprisoned in 1941, if the SS worked starving prisoners to death in only a couple of weeks, this was fine—it made more room for new victims. But by 1942 the war lengthened and the tide began to turn against the Germans. By 1943 orders were given to keep more prisoners alive longer to turn out the desperately needed war materials in the factories by then located in satellite camps or just outside Auschwitz. Unfortunately for the prisoners, by the time this new policy was formulated, many were too malnourished to be saved. It was only after Kolbe's death that as many as thirty-six sub-camps existed within the concentration camp complex, about thirty of them built around factories (including plants of such big German syndicates as I.G. Farbenindustrie, Hermann Göring Werke, Siemens-Schuckert, and many others whose names have been documented). But even when Kolbe first arrived, a chemical plant of I.G. Farbenindustrie was producing synthetic rubber using prisoners as at least part of the labor force. These factories were also built by camp labor.

The forced labor of innocent prisoners was a source of enormous profits for the organizers of mass murder and their industrialist allies. I.G. Farbenindustrie, for example, paid the camp administrators—that is, the SS—4 Marks a day for each skilled laborer, 3 Marks for each unskilled. In a period of only seven months the SS received 12 million Marks from just this one company. At those very low wages, the company's profits must have been tremendous. In addition, the mass murderers and the Reich acquired the goods of the murdered. At war's end, the SS managed to burn twenty-nine of the thirty-five warehouses that stored these blood-tainted items. To mention just one item of thousands, 13,664 carpets were found in the six intact warehouses. Even the hair and the gold teeth of the dead swelled the coffers of the Reich.

Finally, Auschwitz was a place for medical experiments that would have been prohibited as criminal anywhere else. One of the most important of these, carried out by SS doctors under Dr. Carl Clauberg, sought an easy mass sterilization method that would permit biological extermination of entire nations, Slavs in particular, while keeping the present generation alive to work until they were no longer useful.

The prisoners were all Polish the first year (June 1940–1941), so Kolbe, arriving in May 1941 entered a camp composed exclusively of his fellow countrymen. The camp assumed an international character a month after Kolbe's entrance, when transports of Czechoslovakians arrived. These were followed, in July, by the first prisoners of war from the Soviet Union. Recovered scraps of documents mention prisoners of the following nations or bloods: Americans, English, Austrians, Belgians, Bulgarians, Croats, Czechoslovakians, Dutch, French, Germans, Greeks, Gypsies, Hungarians, Italians, Yugoslavians, Lithuanians, Latvians, Norwegians, Poles, Rumanians, Russians, Slovaks, Spaniards, and Turks. Many of these individuals were Jews.

Murder by mass gassings was not going on when Kolbe entered Auschwitz, but it began while he was there in July. The prisoners were unaware of the first incident, however, since the 573 selected prisoners—children and the chronically ill—were shipped to Sonnenstein in Saxony and gassed in a mental hospital there. The gassings of groups at Auschwitz began two to five weeks after Kolbe's death. A "test run" was made on 600 Soviet prisoners of war and 250 invalids from the camp hospital.* Since this mass murder was successful, that same fall another 10,000 Soviet prisoners of war were put to death in the same manner. Of the 13,000 Soviet prisoners on camp rolls, at the final roll call in January 1945 only ninety-seven remained alive. After that the camp was evacuated and as many prisoners killed as possible.

Another group picked out for extermination simply on the basis of nationality, race, or religion was the Gypsies. In April 1943, Hitler ordered the Gypsies of Europe in all territories controlled by the Reich arrested. Men, women, children, and infants were brought to a special satellite camp by Birkenau. Those not already

---

*This took place in the same basement penal area (called the Bunker) where Kolbe had been held—a prison within the prison, for deaths and tortures. There were no large gas chambers and only the one relatively small crematorium. A letter dated August 3, 1942, contracted with the German firm of Topf and Sohne to build four vast crematoria with gas chambers in the complex. In these several million, the largest number Jews, died. Prisoners operated the crematoria and were themselves killed frequently, so as to leave no witnesses to these crimes. October 7, 1944, on a day when seven hundred were to be gassed, these workers revolted and managed before they were killed to burn crematorium number 4 and damage number 3.

dead from conditions there on August 1, 1944, were gassed on that date. Of 20,945 Gypsies on the camp rolls, 2,000 had been sent to other camps; of the rest, there are no known survivors.

Although the few Jews there were singled out for the worst treatment, when Kolbe came to Auschwitz, survivors say, there were not yet many Jewish prisoners. The first specifically Jewish transport would not arrive until March 1942. Consisting of 999 Slovakian Jewish women, it opened the women's camp of the Auschwitz complex. The inhuman medical experiments also did not begin until after Kolbe's death, with SS Commander-in-Chief Heinrich Himmler's order for prisoners to be made "available" to Dr. Clauberg being dated July 7, 1942. This is not to imply things got worse after 1941. Prisoners have testified that the heights of savagery in *individual* acts toward individual prisoners took place in the earliest period, when Kolbe was there. This would jibe with the policy changes that followed realization by the Reich that German labor had to be supplemented by slave labor if Germany was not to lose the war. However, it is somehow callous to even speak of conditions having improved when millions were still to be exterminated as if they were vermin, not human beings. Similarly, there is a lack of proper horror in easy statements that being gassed en masse is "better" than being individually tortured to death. Let it suffice to say that Kolbe was at Auschwitz in a very bad period.

Who died at this core camp while he was there? Kolbe had said, "Poland must expect the worst," and he was right: It was Poland's men and boys—particularly her best and her brightest—who were the principal camp victims. Ethnically, this included not just the Poles but Byelorussians, Ukranians, Lithuanians, and others. (Thirty-five percent of the Polish population was comprised of ethnic minorities when the nation was "reconstituted" after World War I.) Jews, who accounted for ten percent of the nation, were represented in about that percentage when Kolbe was at Auschwitz. Explains Ted Wojtkowski, a survivor: "At that time there were only sporadic transports of the Jews (perhaps 200–300 prisoners). However, they were placed immediately in a Block 13 command and nobody would dare to contact them. Excessive hard labor killed the [majority of] the Jewish prisoners in a short time."

Later, in the total camp complexes—particularly the so-called extermination camp of Birkenau, where individuals were transported for the express purpose of gassing—Poland's Jewish population would be represented by men, women, children, and infants out of all proportion to their numbers. In fact, it is believed that of the estimated half of Poland's six million war dead who were Jews (an estimate including those who died from all causes), a large portion of them died at this one site. By then they were being persecuted not as Poles but as Jews, joining others brought to Auschwitz from all over Europe. This was a vast and varied group ranging from courageous, holy rabbis, such as those of Poznan in Poland, who could have escaped but chose to stay with their congregations; to Berlin humanists who had never entered a synagogue and considered themselves 100 percent German; to those who revered their heritage of Judaism but had added to it, like the Carmelite nuns Edith and Rosa Stein. To this writer, just as it is understandable that indomitably Catholic Poland should be crucified and rise again full of spiritual life, it is poignantly understandable that the Jews, "the chosen people" beloved of God, should have been singled out for the Nazis' inhuman (and ultimately unsuccessful) persecution. Like Christ, the Jews are a sign to the world, a light proclaiming the everlasting spiritual dimension and pilgrimage of man; and it is signs and lights that darkness tries hardest to extinguish.

Soviet citizens, says Gawalewicz, were the second largest group of victims, by nationality, in this camp—an understandable fact when one recalls that an estimated ten million Soviets died in World War II—but they had only begun to come into the camp during Kolbe's last month there.

While there are important reasons to sort the camp's victims into such categories, it is good also to remember that each member of the human family was at Auschwitz as a unique, irreplaceable individual. Each clung, moment by moment, to a priceless personal existence.

Six years later, Ladislaus Swies, a Brother in the Missionary Congregation of the Pallotines, looked back on the day Kolbe and he were in the transport of prisoners from Pawiak to Auschwitz:

On the 28th of May, 1941, the SS loaded 320 prisoners from Pawiak into closed boxcars to deport us to Auschwitz. After the SS men had stuffed us into the windowless cars, a lugubrious silence fell. The crowding and the lack of air in the car made the atmosphere suffocating . . . unbearable. Moreover the knowledge that we were on our way to a concentration camp had everyone sunk in depression.

But suddenly to my surprise and great joy, somebody started singing. Immediately I took up the melody as then did others. I took an interest in who had started the singing and learned that it was Father Maximilian Kolbe, the Franciscan founder of Niepokalanow. . . .

Under the influence of Father Maximilian's religious and patriotic songs and narrations, we actually cheered up, forgetting our sad destiny.

The Nazi version of that destiny was outlined for them the same evening when, snapped at by angry dogs and whipped by snarling guards, they were chased in terror through the sinister gates with their ironic sign: "Arbeit Macht Frei" ("Work leads to Freedom"). Brought to a standstill on the parade ground, the mass of prisoners heard a roll call of their names for the first and almost last time in Auschwitz. As each man's name was called, he had to pass along a gauntlet of SS men who had whips in hand. The running prisoner was whipped, kicked, and cursed. Then he was added to the orderly ranks forming under supervision of SS officers such as Palitsch,* who by the following year would boast that he personally had shot 25,000 men. Standing at attention, the prisoners then heard the plan for their future from either Kommandant Höss† or one of his sub-führers:

Let me tell you that you have not arrived at a health spa, but a German concentration camp. You will find only one exit — the crematorium chimney. If you don't like the sound of this, you can leave at once by

---

*Auschwitz survivor Ted Wojtkowski recounts (with satisfaction at the apparent justice of it) that the heartless Palitsch came to his well-earned downfall at the hands of the SS when he fell in love with a woman prisoner, either a Jewish or Gypsy girl. Imprisoned for a time because of this, he was later demoted and sent into combat, where he vanished. Apparently because of his disgrace, his wife jumped out a second-story window to her death.

† Höss, convicted of crimes against humanity, was hung at Auschwitz following the war.

throwing yourself on the electric fences. Now if any of you are Jews, you have the right to live no longer than two weeks; priests, one month; the rest of you, three months.

After this welcome, the shocked, exhausted, and hungry prisoners were herded into a too-small, fetid hall and locked in for the night. For lack of air, some fainted. Kolbe's name in the roll call of new inmates had been noticed by the camp. Holding a rather high Polish government post in 1939, Francis Mleczko was a natural Gestapo target. As a prisoner who had been in Auschwitz since 1940, he recalls:

> From mouth to mouth passed the words, "Father Maximilian Kolbe is among us." Men shook their heads, "Even him! How cruel these Nazis are." And we wondered what dire things were going on in Poland. At the same time, we were glad to have such a real man, a fighter — a fighter for truth — with us.

The following morning Kolbe, barely recovered from pneumonia, and all his fellow prisoners were taken to icy showers. The warm vest, the suit, and other items that the Brothers had scurried to provide were taken from him to swell the warehouses of the SS. In exchange he, like every prisoner, received thin blue-and-gray denim, horizontally striped pants and shirt taken from some dead victim, sometimes still bearing the bloodstains from his death. Their heads were shaved. They were not tatooed in 1941 (this practice was instituted later by the methodical Germans, not only to foil escapees, but because the corpses' garments were sometimes so tattered or destroyed that the prisoners' identification number on sleeve and pants could not be read). Each was given a number, however, and it was by this—not his name—that he would be called from now on. Kolbe became 16,670. Mleczko, who today lives in Webster, Massachusetts, explains:

> When at that time he got the number 16,670, that meant the camp had received that many prisoners (minus the capos, who got the numbers 1 through 30). In reality, there were probably closer to 8,000 in the camp. The difference between the 16,000 some admitted and the 8,000 resulted from the numbers who had already been killed since the camp opened in June 1940. I don't say died, you notice, but killed. They were

killed with baseball bats, killed with rods, killed by vermin, killed by hunger. . . . It was awful . . . awful. One needs the pen of a Dante, one needs a genius to describe this misery, this hell. . . .

The new prisoners were parceled out among the plain but substantial-looking two-story brick barracks called blocks (eventually there were twenty-eight), all but the first built by camp labor. Each of these held at least six hundred men (some estimates go up by two hundred or more). Kolbe was assigned to Block 18. There were at that time no bunks; the prisoners slept on bagged straw spread side by side on the floor, usually two or more to one pallet.

Henry Sienkiewicz lived in Block 18. Sienkiewicz, a twenty-four-year-old Polish soldier who had not surrendered to the Germans, was caught in April 1940, tortured for a month or two by the Gestapo in Pawiak's cellars, sentenced to death by the German army, and then suddenly reprieved to Auschwitz. Number 2,714, he would survive and become a forest ranger. He recalls:

> I had often heard of Father Maximilian Kolbe, founder of Niepokalanow, before the war. Now he was suddenly, at the end of May 1941, sleeping next to me. We became very close during the five weeks he was in Block 18, and even after that no day ever passed during which I did not see him.
>
> I noticed how, making the sign of the cross, he knelt at night and began to pray. I tried to persuade him not to expose himself so openly to the punishment of the capo or the SS (praying was strictly forbidden). He listened to my warning, then replied gently, "Go to sleep, my son, because tomorrow you have a hard day's work ahead of you and you need to rest. I'm already an old man* so I'll stay up and pray for you. I came here to share with you the sad fate of the concentration camp."

Each prisoner who arrived was also assigned a work detail. These could vary from cushy indoor jobs like work in the warehouse filled with liquor and delights for their women—goods stolen from all over Europe—that served the SS guards as a PX, to certain-death jobs like pushing the huge cement road roller under orders of the bestial Krankemann,† a capo so evil he eventually even fell afoul of the SS, who forced him to hang himself. The

---

*He was forty-seven.

†Some sources give the name as Krunkemann.

warehouse and other comparatively safe jobs went to those who
spoke fluent German. But not to priests.

Why did the Nazis hate priests so? There can no more be a
rational answer to that question than one can rationally explain
Nazi anti-Semitism, which goes deeper than any "national scape-
goat" or political stratagem straight to the heart of evil. But a
memory of Henry Sienkiewicz will give cause for reflection:

> Right after my arrival at Auschwitz, a young priest was murdered. His
> body, in a cassock, was laid out on a wheelbarrow. A mock funeral was
> staged by the SS men, who forced several priests and a few Jews to
> sing funeral hymns as they followed another cassock-dressed priest. He
> wore a hat turned upside down, a straw rope was tied about his neck,
> and they made him carry a broom as his cross. We were forced to
> stand there looking at this mockery while the SS men jeered at us hop-
> ing to arouse fear, to subjugate us: "Your god and your ruler: that's us,
> the SS and the capos and the camp commander. There is no other
> god!"

To some extent, priests and Jews were lumped together in the
SS mind. Mieczyslaus Koscielniak, who became a good friend of
Kolbe's, remembers an incident that explains the connection:

> In may 1941 we were working in a torn-down house when one of
> the prisoners found a crucifix. SS Storch got ahold of it and he called
> Father Nieweglewski.
>
> "What is this?" he asks the priest. Father remains silent, but the guard
> insists until he says, "Christ on the cross."
>
> Then Storch jeers: "Why you fool, that's the Jew who, thanks to the
> silly ideals which he preached and you fell for, got you into this camp.
> Don't you understand? He's one of the Jewish ringleaders! A Jew is a
> Jew and will always be a Jew! How can you believe in such an enemy?"
>
> Father Nieweglewski is silent.
>
> Then Storch says, "You know, if you'll trample this Jew" — and he
> throws the crucifix on the sand — I'll get you transferred to a better job."
>
> When the priest refused, the SS man and the capo threw him a cou-
> ple of times on the crucifix; then they beat him so badly that, shortly
> after, he died.

Such martyrdoms were not unusual. Father Joseph Kowalski was
doomed because he would not step on a rosary crucifix; Father

Peter Dankowski, from Zakopane, was tortured and killed on Good Friday by a capo who sneered, "Jesus Christ was killed today and you also will perish this day."

How did the priests react? Survivor Father Conrad Szweda, a twenty-four-year-old associate pastor who was one of the first Auschwitz prisoners, says:

> We were in constant terror. It was like a psychosis. What were they doing this to us for? We could not even trust one another because sometimes there were spies among the prisoners. Religious practices were all forbidden. Even prayer was not allowed on pain of severe beating or being put to death. We priests still got together occasionally to pray in common, but no one dared single himself out to deliver a sermon, which could have marked him for death. The exception, of course, after his arrival, was Father Kolbe, who said he was willing to put his life on the line to bring others to Christ.
>
> There were a few sad cases of human weakness among the terror-stricken clergy, but still, granting our constant fear, I can say wherever there was mistreatment and death there were priests praying, interceding, hearing confessions, encouraging, and lifting up others' souls. I remember once when about five hundred patients were being led from the hospital to the gas chambers. They didn't know where they were going and at first neither did we. But after the first ones were taken to the underground bunkers, our eyes were opened. We realized they were going to their death and therefore as priests we began to absolve them all and to try to dispose them. That, to me, was a very great thing — that God did not leave people without shepherds even in such situations.

Jewish Auschwitz survivor Eddie Gastfriend agrees with Father Szweda that most priests managed to hold onto their ideals and not become brutalized. Interviewed by newspaperman Tom Fox, Gastfriend, a Pole who is now a merchant in Philadelphia, says:

> There were many priests in Auschwitz. They wore no collars, but you knew they were priests by their manner and their attitude, especially toward Jews. They were so gentle, so loving.
>
> Those of us Jews who came into contact with priests, such as Father Kolbe (I didn't know him personally, but I heard stories about him), felt it was a moving time — a time when a covenant in blood was written between Christians and Jews. . . .

This, then, was the situation at Auschwitz: Jews and priests struggling to maintain their humanity against the terrors without and the knee-shaking terror within, while the SS singled them out to be not just killed but spiritually crushed. In this atmosphere, frail-looking Maximilian Kolbe reported to his first work squad. Henry Sienkiewicz describes his older friend's first assignment.

> During his first days in the camp, Father Maximilian was assigned to the squad where the priests and Jews worked.* They were building [a wall by] the crematorium. Once Father was pushing a wheelbarrow full of gravel. Because the wheelbarrow was a big one but its wheel was small, this made the work all the harder. The task was beyond his human strength, so I wanted to help him. I suggested he stop for a few minutes and I'd make a few trips in his place.
>
> Unfortunately, the capo noticed this and because we had talked to each other, he gave us each ten blows with a stick. During my ten blows from the capo, I was yelling bloody murder, but Father did not even utter a groan, although he must have suffered atrociously.
>
> Then the capo said, "You want to help him. All right, we'll let you work together" and he ordered Father Maximilian to push the wheelbarrow already full of gravel with me sitting on top all the way to the dumping site and then back again empty, with me in it. He had to do this twice and I had to do it once with him on top of the gravel.
>
> To console me, he said "Hank, let's offer all this suffering for the Mother of God. Let them see that we are her servants."

George Bielecki, who had been at Auschwitz since October 1940, is another survivor who recalls Kolbe at work:

> He and I worked together in May or June 1941. We were bringing sand up from the Sola River. This was some of the camp's heaviest work, so our squad had a very hard time indeed. The work itself was very painful; we were lightly and very insufficiently dressed, and yet we had to wade into the cold water to dig the sand. In addition the guards

---

*Father Szweda gives slightly different testimony: he says Jews and priests were separated from the rest of the prisoners on their first day, but also from each other. (Of course, prisoners may have been treated differently at different times.) Szweda remembers that Jews were "beaten to unconsciousness," then put in what was termed the "Block of Death," a special command where conditions were worse than anywhere else. Priests were put to hard labor under harsher conditions than other prisoners, but they were spared the initial beating reserved for Jews.

beat us cruelly or sometimes killed prisoners outright.

From the first time I saw Father Maximilian I was struck by his dignity and calm, so different from others. In spite of the terrible conditions and bad treatment, he never complained nor did he curse. Instead he tried to comfort the other prisoners and lift our spirits.

During the three weeks we worked together, I sometimes saw the capo beat Father Kolbe with a big stick. Each time, Father Kolbe took it without a murmur.

Although Kolbe never complained or mentioned any beatings to others, Father Szweda has collected some details of what was probably his most harrowing two weeks in Auschwitz's work squads. Szweda says:

> The new arrivals had seen the Jews in their group ordered to step forward and then beaten to the point of unconsciousness. Now, after a few days work at heavy labor in the gravel pits, the priests, too, were ordered to step forward. Fritsch personally ordered, "Priest-Schwein, follow me!" Paling, they followed, the mud from the gravel pit drying on their uniforms as they marched. Fritsch turned them over to the so-called Babice command.* The capo of this work squad was known as "Krott the Bloody," because of his record of annihilating prisoners. Fritsch presented the priests to him with the remark, "Here are the parasites of society. Teach them how to work!" Smiling cynically, the capo replied offhandedly, "I'll get along with them." At once he started them marching the four kilometers to the work site, where they would join other prisoners digging out trunks and cutting trees, which they then used to fence the swampy meadow.

> The work was done at a run, with foremen stationed every several yards to beat any prisoner—especially priests, for whom Krott had a special ferocity—who slowed down. It was a real Way of the Cross. For Father Maximilian it lasted two weeks. He was singled out to carry loads that were two or three times what nonpriests carried—and carrying anything, especially at a run, was difficult over the uneven ground of the swamp. If he paused to rest, he was beaten with sticks. Fellow priests who saw him bleeding wanted to help, but he told them—usually with a smile—"Don't expose yourselves to a beating. The Immaculata is helping me. I'll get along."

---

*Named, perhaps, for an area bordering the camp.

One day was especially dreadful for Kolbe. The bloody capo selected him to be the day's special victim and tortured him as a bird of prey would a hapless mouse. Krott himself loaded Father Maximilian's back with the heaviest branches, then ordered him to run. When the priest fell, Krott kicked him mercilessly in the face and stomach, shouting, "You don't want to work, you drone! I'll show you what work means." ...He ordered Kolbe to lie across a stump. Then from among the guards Krott summoned the strongest and ordered them to give the innocent priest fifty lashes.

Afterwards Father Kolbe couldn't even move. So Krott threw him into the mud and threw the branches on top of him. When it was time to march back to the camp, Father Maximilian was still in such a state that others had to carry him. The next day he was taken to the camp hospital.

Szweda's account now becomes first-hand:

I was then an orderly in the camp hospital, working in the section reserved for infectious diseases. When I learned that Father Kolbe was in the hospital, I went right away to see how he was. His face was all bruised, his eyes lusterless, and fever burned his body to the point that his swollen tongue couldn't move and his voice died out in his throat. But in spite of the extreme fever, he wasn't delirious.

I couldn't get myself transferred to that section to take care of him, but I got someone to give him special attention. After a few days he was a little recuperated, but the pneumonia was not over, the fever continued. His attitude in the face of suffering was a marvel to the prisoner doctors and nurses. He conducted himself with virility and with complete acceptance of the will of God. He often said, "For Jesus Christ I'm ready to suffer more than this. The Immaculata is helping me."

For some inexplicable reason, even after the pneumonia crisis passed, the fever remained [this may have indicated tuberculosis again or the common camp disease typhus]. He was moved to the area where I worked — communicable diseases — and put in a ward with those suspected of typhus. Now I could see him more easily.

Because with a high fever one suffers a lot without any liquid, I brought him once a cup of tea, carefully saved, so he could moisten his feverish lips. I could see how parched he was. To my astonishment, he refused to take it. "I can't," he said, indicating the other patients. "They don't have any; let's give it to them." To console me, he added, "Don't worry, I'll get along somehow. The Immaculata is helping me still."

When I asked if he'd like to be transferred out of the typhus ward, he said no, he'd prefer to remain there so he could comfort the patients and bless the dead as they were carried out. He had the lower bunk by the door and as each dead man was carried past, the individual received his blessing and conditional absolution. In regard to the living sick and suffering, he took up his mission as pastor of souls. Drawing on his rich experience, he told anecdotes that lifted their spirits, led common prayer, and gave conferences on the Immaculata, whom he loved with the simplicity of a child. At night under the cover of dark prisoners came to his bed begging him to hear their confessions or seeking comfort. The other patients loved him so much that he was universally called "our little father."

I must say too that, in spite of his fevered condition, it was he who comforted me. When after my day's work I came to him, he pressed me to his chest as a mother her child. Sometimes I was deeply depressed and complained that I could not go on.

"But what if God wants you to live and survive this camp?" he asked. He held out Mary to me saying, "She is the consoler of the afflicted who listens to everyone, helps everyone who calls on her." I especially found comfort in his urging, "Take Christ's hand in one of yours and Mary's in the other. Now even if you are in darkness you can go forward with the confidence of a child guided by its parents."

I owe a great deal to his motherly heart.

14

Some of His Friends

ONRAD SZWEDA met Kolbe in Auschwitz, drawn at once to the older man who preached when no one else dared. In the short while they were together, the young priest came to love and revere the older one, whom he believed to be a saint. One of his sons at Niepokalanow characterized Kolbe as one "with a real understanding of how to be someone's friend." The truth of that showed in Auschwitz. Wherever Kolbe went, as Szweda says, "like a magnet, he drew people to him."

This was true in Block 18, in his first work squads, and in the hospital. It was also true when he was assigned after the hospital to the invalids block, then to Block 14, where he cleaned latrines, shoveled manure, and peeled potatoes in the camp kitchen.

Such a universal response to a stranger was unusual in the death camp. A few brief comments from survivors may explain why:

"Camp life was inhuman, unnatural—you dared not trust anyone because there were spies even among the prisoners."

"Everyone is an egoist at heart. With men being killed on every side, you hope the others will die and you will live."

"People's animal instincts were aroused because of the hunger. Everyone was driven by the need to eat. There was a general feeling that the whole world was perishing in mutual hatred."

"Each of us thought only of this: to live! Nobody interested himself in his neighbor."

"I remember the fellow physician working in the camp hospital who growled to me, 'Let them all drop dead! I don't care. All that matters is that *I* survive!' "

Ted Wojtkowski, who today lives near Chicago, remembers a chilling example of the lengths to which the almost universal self-absorption could go:

It was a summer Sunday. Everyone breathed a little, because that day the guards took a rest and so we could too. Then suddenly everyone was ordered back out on the parade ground. The numbers from roll call hadn't tallied. One prisoner was missing. So we thousands would stand in the summer sun until he was found unconscious, dead, or hiding somewhere. We stood while the guards turned the Blocks inside and out. Then we stood while they searched the rest of the camp. Hour after hour: I was boiling and my only day of rest was passing. After a while I began to hope they would find the guy so I could be left in peace. As usual, some of the malnourished men (I had a warehouse job where I could filch food) dropped in the ranks. Maybe some died. No one could help them or lift them up to see. Finally it was almost evening. I was in a rage by then. All at once the order is given for *us* to comb the camp. Ranks are broken and everyone begins turning the place inside and out all over again. Me, I snuck into the latrine and cleaned up a bit. It wasn't long with all those prisoners looking for him before the poor devil was found, stark naked, hidden under a pile of corpses waiting to be carried outside for disposal.

Betrayed by a fellow victim. The thought of those two face to face chills the blood. Of course, concern for others was not totally dead. The same man who has the courage and honesty to reveal that he momentarily wished an escapee would be found so he could get his own tired, burning head and blistered feet out of the sun knew four other prisoners who planned—and successfully executed—a daring escape, which they invited him to share. Because he had a family who would bear the reprisals, Ted says matter-of-factly that he refused. Nor did he squeal on his friends, although their deed endangered him by association. Another example of caring is related by survivor Jan Dudzinski. He recounts how Polish doctors saved his life by checking him out of the hospital before each count of those who had been there too long (they were murdered by injection or later gassed) and checked him in again the next day until they healed his frostbite. But the general tone of "Every man for himself" was strong.

Kolbe, who had written that "evil is of its essence a denial of love," entered this dog-eat-dog world like a neon sign proclaiming, "You are your brother's keeper." He intended to use every suffering that came his way, not only to show his love for God by his willingness to suffer for his faith, but to help his fellow prisoners. Convinced that all men are somehow mysteriously linked in God so that what one suffers can be offered for another's benefit, Kolbe tried mystically through his sufferings offered wholeheartedly to God and by his fearless preaching, conferences, hearing of confessions, and complete sharing of himself and his meager material resources to turn Auschwitz inmates from dogs into brothers.

To a greater degree than their brothers and sisters, Christian saints can draw on Jesus' promise in John 15 that those who keep the commandments of love shall receive "all you ask the Father in my name." To believers this explains why, in a place where millions perished without a trace, so many of Maximilian Kolbe's friends survived.

Let them tell you about their extraordinary friend. Joseph Stemler, director of the Polish Education Department, was sent to Auschwitz in April of 1941. He writes:

> Morally, things had really broken down. The struggle to conserve one's life had assumed a form so brutal that it was very rare for a prisoner to aid another. I could name, for instance, a former public prosecutor who stole another man's bread at night.

> I had known [Kolbe] briefly before. I met him, in fact, in 1938 at the conference of newspaper editors. Many were attracted to him by his youthful smile and his joy. He was one of those who have absolutely nothing artificial about them. Far from taking pride in his expertise in the editorial field, he seemed somewhat embarrassed that it was he who knew the answers to so many questions.

> Our next meeting was under far different circumstances. It happened in Auschwitz around the end of June or the beginning of July 1941. It was after the evening roll call. Exhausted and dying of hunger, I was on

my way back to Block 8 when unexpectedly in front of me a guard appeared. Yelling and menacing me with his cudgel, he rushed me off to one side of the assembly ground where two lines of other prisoners stood waiting. The SS then chased us all the way to the hospital Block, where we were ordered to carry corpses to the crematorium.

I wasn't a young man — had even fought in World War I — but I had never touched a corpse. Now before me was my first. A young fellow, completely nude, his belly torn, his legs bloody while his contorted hands and his face spoke clearly of his agonizing suffering. I couldn't move even one step toward him. The guard began to scream at me but then a calm voice said, "Let's pick him up, my brother."

For a fraction of a second I thought I knew that voice. Filled with repugnance, somehow I took hold of a bloody leg while my companion took the corpse by the shoulder and we deposited it, as directed, with a second body in a kind of trough-like receptacle usually used for slaughtered animals. This we were to carry to the crematorium.

I was too upset to function. My arms seemed to be failing me, my wooden shoes would no longer stay on my feet. I thought it would be better if it were I being carried out so gruesomely. Suddenly at my shoulder I heard the calm but moving voice of my companion: "Holy Mary . . . pray for us."

Something like an electric current passed through my failing limbs and suddenly I felt strong. Now with vigor I carried the strange casket.

We reached the crematorium, a low building with a flat roof and a tall chimney from which the wind swept away a pestilential smoke.

There we had to stack up the two corpses with others after having given the guards the number written with a certain type of pencil on the chests of the dead. An error could provoke a fatal incident. Some family would receive notice of the death of a near one while the person still lived. One was obliged to witness the macabre catafalque made of a great movable grate over the flames where the poor corpses of the dead prisoners were burning.

[In my horror] I was at that moment prey for delirium, unconscious. . . . Turning away with my companion, I was trembling all over. My legs were becoming rigid; then my companion very gently pushed the container which had held the corpses and with it pushed me.

As soon as we crossed the threshold of the crematorium I heard his clear, low voice say, "Rest in Peace." Moments later he whispered "And the Word was made Flesh."

Only then did I recognize that my companion was the Franciscan from Niepokalanow, Father Kolbe.

Later, Stemler came down with diarrhea—usually fatal to prisoners. Accepted into the hospital, he recalled later:

I was in the bunk next to the famous socialist writer Barlicki. John Pozaryski of the Society of Authors told me Father Kolbe was in the ward. He had the bottom bunk near the door. Following the example of many others, under cover of night, I crawled on the floor to his bed.

He greeted me in a way that was very moving. We exchanged a few words on our impressions of the terrible crematorium. Then we remained in silence. I was contemplating his emaciated face, beardless and difficult to recognize. Only his eyes more than ever shone, but perhaps that was from fever. I didn't want to tire him and yet I wanted to tell him so many things.

It was he who encouraged me [to talk], and we finished by his hearing my confession. My feelings were so unhappy and desperate. I wanted to live!

His words, on the other hand, were simple and profound. He urged me to have firm faith in the victory of good.

"Hate is not creative; only love is creative," he whispered, pressing my hand warmly in his ardor. "These sufferings will not cause us to crumble but will help us more and more to become stronger. They are necessary, even—together with the sacrifices of others—so that the ones who come after us will be happy."

The way he continued to clasp my hand so warmly and the way he pointed everything toward the mercy of God heartened me. Only when he urged me to pardon the oppressors and return good for evil did I react rebelliously. In the successive days I returned to his bed. We spoke without words. In the nights I led to him other prisoners who desired spiritual comfort.

I remember the day when I saw him for the last time. This came about because of the hospital police. The capo of the hospital Block was a man given to frenzied rages. With a cynical smile he ran from bed to bed, feigning to be a doctor, taking temperatures but never looking at the thermometers, scrutinizing instead the faces of the prisoner patients. The artificer was looking for intellectuals. Anyone whose face seemed that of a man of culture this dwarfish man hated.

After his rounds that same day, both Father Maximilian and I were thrown out of the hospital. Waiting under guard to be given clothes and a new block assignment, we were outside between Blocks 21 and 22. I was not positioned near Father Kolbe, but I could see he was watching me insistently. He seemed to want to tell me something. I profited by some distraction among the guards and moved over to him. He squeezed my hand warmly and said to me in his clear voice: "I commend you to the protection of the Immaculate." Scarcely had he pronounced these words than a guard's yell rushed me back to my place.

I continued to watch Father Kolbe. It was the last time and so this is how I remember him today, as I saw him in those moments: slightly tilted shaved head with hints of baldness, deep-set eyes shining like live coals, regular nose, cheeks that looked more hollow because of whiskers not shaved for several weeks, youthful lips with a forgiving smile on them. From the short hospital smock stuck out thin arms and terribly meager legs. Suddenly, as I was watching him, the guards called my number. I had to go.

"So long," I shouted toward Father Maximilian. And as I was led away I could see that he continued to accompany me with his glance and his smile.

Stemler was an intellectual. Another of Kolbe's friends was a tailor, thirty-six-year-old Alexander Dziuba, who had been in Auschwitz since September 1940. He remembers:

I once heard another priest say, "Oh God, if you really exist, punish these criminals!" You never heard anything like that from Father Kolbe. He had such heroic trust in God that he saw God's finger in every event. If a prisoner was to die, he would [still] say, "That's God's will." He himself was totally abandoned to God. I recall that he once said he would not hesitate to give his life for God. And I noticed too that he never schemed or organized things so as to get something to eat for himself, to obtain better clothing, an easier work detail. . . . He was concerned—I heard him say so myself—"only for my soul and my faith."

I owe to him that I am still alive, that I was able to hold out and lived to be liberated. In that period the capos and guards often beat me during my work hours. I began to feel, why not end it all by throwing myself on the wires [the electric fences] the way other prisoners did. So one day, in a fit of despair, I rushed for the fence but I was seized, made to turn back, and given fifty blows in punishment.

Father Kolbe heard about it. He talked to me and calmed me down

The expanded chapel at Niepokalanow.

Typesetting at Niepokalanow, where the Brothers worked in shifts to produce eleven different publications.

Brothers working on the daily newspaper at Niepokalanow in the late 1930s.

A German soldier escorting the Franciscan Brothers who were taken into custody by the Nazis during World War II and sent to an internment camp at Amtitz. Only a handful of Brothers remained at the friary, under close supervision by the Nazis.

The dread fence in the concentration camp of Auschwitz. Suicide on it was common.

Drawing of Kolbe volunteering to take the place of a prisoner condemned to die in reprisal for an escapee who had not been found. By Polish artist Prof. Miecislaus Koscielniak, a fellow prisoner of Kolbe's at Auschwitz.

Auschwitz's "Block of Death," where Kolbe died.

Kolbe in 1940.

Francis Gajowniczek, the
man whom Kolbe replaced
in the "hunger bunker."

Saint Peter's in Rome, at the beatification of Kolbe on October 17, 1971. It was
here that he was subsequently canonized on October 10, 1982.

beatings of the capos and guards. I examined those who reported sick and determined who got hospital care. Daily I observed the poor creatures crowding into the hospital, each shoving and straining to save his life.

In this formidable throng my attention was drawn to a prisoner about my age who never pushed. His whole conduct was so modest and humble that he seemed almost to apologize for living. He invariably tried to wait until the two hundred to five hundred and one day one thousand others crowded in. When I called him out to be examined (he was suffering and fevered from his lungs), I said to him, "You know you're so weak it would be best to admit you to the hospital; therefore, I'll assign you . . ." he interrupted me to plead, "I think I'll be all right a little longer — why not take that one over there," pointing to some other half-starved soul.

Amazed, I shrugged, "Well, if you don't want to, at least take this," and I gave him some medicine. In view of the general animal instinct of self-preservation so evident in everyone else (the main motive for any camp action was generally to hold on to life), his desire to sacrifice himself for others surprised and intrigued me. I observed him narrowly on those occasions. His expression was so different. Because they were trying to survive at any cost, all the prisoners had wildly roving eyes watching in every direction for trouble or the ready clubs. Kolbe, alone, had a calm straightforward look, the look of a thoughtful man, a profound thinker, of one not much concerned with protecting himself. Besides his humility and simplicity, he was obviously a man of great culture and knowledge. It seemed to me his uncommon love of neighbor was no momentary impulse of the sort one sees frequently enough, but something profoundly rooted in his personality. (Later, in one of our philosophical discussions on religion, he told me that every man has a purpose in life. His life, he said, he had consecrated to doing good to all men.)

After his refusal to let me admit him to the hospital had happened on several occasions, I finally said to him as he was arguing for my taking someone else, "Listen, if you don't go to bed, you'll die."

"I think I'll hold out," he answered.

"What kind of role are you playing, that of a saint?" I snapped. "Are you perhaps a religious?"

"Well, yes, I'm a Catholic priest," he admitted. So I said, "Well, if you want to be a saint, that's too bad. There's really no sense in that. . . ."

But I admired him. Spiritually, in spite of his physical suffering, he was completely healthy, serene and balanced in disposition, and extraordinary in character. Everyday I met hundreds of prisoners from all walks of life — priests, professors, princes, artists — I never saw another like him in Auschwitz or outside Auschwitz, for that matter.

I asked him once if he still believed that God looks out for us. He tried fervently to show me this is the case and proposed that we meet in the Birkenalei [Birch Alley] to walk and talk sometime. I decided to accept. There one day he said, "Doctor, you've done so much for me, I'd like to repay you in some way."

Though I was very impressed by his sense of gratitude, still I had to smile. "How could you reciprocate?" I asked him. "I have enough to eat. I'm comfortable. What could you give me?"

"Now that it's Easter time," he answered, "maybe you would like a little spiritual comfort?"

Since I didn't understand what he meant, he continued, "Maybe go to confession?"

"How could I?" I replied "since I no longer have any belief. Besides, I'm a Protestant by background, not a Catholic."

After I thanked him for his offer that I could not accept, we discussed religion, he trying to show me I did believe in God, and this discussion, like each one that I had with him, gave me great satisfaction because of his integrity. To this day I feel great gratitude and admiration toward Father Kolbe.

Sigmund Gorson today is the host of a television program in Wilmington, Delaware. Although he has written and spoken on life in Auschwitz, he regards his memories of Kolbe as "so personal, so precious" that he has never included anything on the Catholic priest he calls "a prince among men." He breaks this silence now because he appears to be the only one left of the Polish Jews who knew Kolbe well in Auschwitz.

I was from a beautiful home where love was the key word. My parents were well-off and well-educated. But my three beautiful sisters, my mother — an attorney educated at the University of Paris — my father, grandparents — all perished. I am the sole survivor. To be a child from such a wonderful home and then suddenly find oneself utterly alone, as I did at age thirteen, in this hell, Auschwitz, has an effect on one others can hardly comprehend. Many of us youngsters lost hope, especially when the Nazis showed us pictures of what they said was the bombing of New York City. Without hope, there was no chance to survive, and many boys my age ran onto the electric fences. I was always looking for some link with my murdered parents, trying to find a friend of my father's, a neighbor — someone in that mass of humanity who had known them so I would not feel so alone.

And that is how Kolbe found me wandering around, so to speak, looking for someone to connect with. He was like an angel to me. Like a mother hen, he took me in his arms. He used to wipe away my tears. I believe in God more since that time. Because of the deaths of my parents I had been asking, "Where is God?" and had lost faith. Kolbe gave me that faith back.

He knew I was a Jewish boy. That made no difference. His heart was bigger than persons — that is, whether they were Jewish, Catholic, or whatever. He loved everyone. He dispensed love and nothing but love. For one thing, he gave away so much of his meager rations that to me it was a miracle he could live. Now it is easy to be nice, to be charitable, to be humble, when times are good and peace prevails. For someone to be as Father Kolbe was in that time and place — I can only say the way he was is beyond words.

I am a Jew by my heritage as the son of a Jewish mother, and I am of the Jewish faith and very proud of it. And not only did I love Maximilian Kolbe very, very much in Auschwitz, where he befriended me, but I will love him until the last moments of my life.

Mieczyslaus Koscielniak, an artist with a degree in philosophy and letters, arrived May 3, 1941, in a transport of three hundred political prisoners, only six of whom survived. He has done many pictures portraying concentration camp life and still has his bloodstained prisoner's uniform with his number, 15,261, the three-cornered emblem of the political prisoners, and the letter P (for Pole). Koscielniak was introduced to Kolbe on the Feast of Corpus Christi, June 12.

I looked at him carefully out of curiosity. Although his hair was cut very short, I could see he was turning gray. He was not tall, very skinny, and slightly round-shouldered. What impressed me especially were his calm and his smile. He was a good companion as well as an exemplary religious and extraordinary man.

Cautiously, in order not to attract attention to ourselves, we sat on some beams and bricks ready for construction. Kolbe began to speak in a subdued voice about the feast day, about God's greatness, and the suffering that we were being permitted to endure. We hung on every word that reminded us we might survive this horrible camp.

He urged us to persevere courageously. "Do not break down morally," he pleaded, promising that God's justice exists and would eventually defeat the Nazis. Listening to him intently, we forgot for the time our hunger and degradation. He made us see that our souls were not dead, our dignity as Catholics and Poles not destroyed. Uplifted in spirit, we returned to our Blocks repeating his words, "We will not break down, we will survive for sure, they will not kill the Polish spirit in us."

It is hard to believe now that I was on a first-name basis with such a great spirit, that he actually came to me for a favor. "Our life here is very uncertain," he said. "One by one we are taken to the crematorium — maybe I'll be going too; but meanwhile, would you draw me a couple of little pictures?" He wanted one of Jesus and one of Our Lady to whom he said, "I have such great devotion." I drew these pictures for him on paper the size of postage stamps. He wanted them that size because he had a hidden pocket sewed inside his rather wide belt and he tucked them in there. Later when he lost these pictures, I made a second set.

At Niepokalanow Maximilian Kolbe had tried to build "a school for saints"; Koscielniak's testimony indicates that at Auschwitz he did the same:

Although it could have cost him his life or severe beatings, he courageously gathered us secretly together almost every day through June and July in order to instruct us. His words meant a great deal to us as he spoke with great faith about the saint whose feast was that day and what had happened to him or her. He spoke with special ardor of the martyrs who had sacrificed themselves totally for God's cause. I particularly recall his fervent invitation on Pentecost to persevere and not grow disheartened as he assured us that, although not all would survive, all of us would conquer.

Like all the Poles in the field of communications who didn't get out of Poland or collaborate with the Nazis, Joseph Cyankiewicz was sent to Auschwitz. He recalls:

I used to meet Brother Lawrence Podwapinski at the monthly meetings of the Polish Association of Newspaper and Magazine Publishers. He was the representative for Niepokalanow's publications. At the Association's convention in 1938, he brought Father Maximilian with him. I was immediately fascinated by the extraordinary appearance of Father Kolbe — the spirituality of his face full of dignity and serenity and adorned by a beautiful beard. After just a short conversation, I came away believing here was a true *hominem fortem* with a sublime spirit.

At Auschwitz I was working in the Kartoflarnia — that is, "the potato place" — so called because that's all that was cooked there. Almost two hundred of us were working very hard under very strict discipline. One day, shortly before I was kicked out of the kitchen squad, a newcomer joined us. It was Father Kolbe. He recognized me immediately because I hadn't become skin and bones yet, having only been imprisoned a short time (actually, as number 13,163, he had been there longer than Kolbe, but kitchen work was less debilitating than hard labor and he had not been giving away part of his rations). I didn't recognize Father Maximilian at all. He had changed greatly: his beard was gone, his face emaciated, and his eyes tired. In spite of my own misfortunes, it hurt me to see such a venerable man so reduced.

In the afternoon we were given a cup of soup with only some small potatoes or other tasteless tuber in it, and without any of the fat destined for the soup because the guards stole, instead of using, it. Extremely hungry and exhausted, all of us awaited impatiently the watery food. Father Kolbe took his and, having crossed himself, began to eat. Immediately a tough young prisoner swaggered over and jeered, "Hey there, old man, what are you doing eating? You're almost done for! Give that to me!" And with an insolent laugh he reached toward the soup. To my astonishment, Father Maximilian handed the food to this bandit. I marveled to those sitting next to me, "We've got another Saint Martin in our midst." We all agreed giving away his food like this showed superhuman courage. Maybe I could have given a little bit of my food to my dearest friend to save his life, but never *all* my soup.

Henry Sienkiewicz was the younger man who slept next to Kolbe when the priest first arrived in Auschwitz. Sienkiewicz, even after Kolbe was in other blocks and work squads, never let a day go by without seeing his friend. He remembers visiting him in the hospital and noting without surprise that, "Father had won all hearts." He also recalls that Kolbe, who showed such tender concern for the sick at Niepokalanow, said he was grateful to God to

be in the hospital because "the sick need prayers and comforting."
He did not mention the terrible beating he had suffered to get
there. Henry says:

> Living day after day as he did hand in hand with God, he seemed to
> have inside him a kind of [spiritual] magnet by which he attracted us to
> himself, to God, and to Our Lady. He kept insisting that God is good and
> merciful. He would have liked to convert the entire camp — including the
> Nazis. Not only did he pray for them, he exhorted *us* to pray for their
> conversion.
>
> I remember how he gave his own wooden shoes, which were still in
> good condition, to another prisoner, taking that fellow's worn clogs for
> himself.
>
> Once I was going to do heavy labor. That morning before I left, Fa-
> ther Maximilian handed me what was about a quarter of his daily bread
> ration. I knew that he had been badly beaten and was exhausted, so I
> was astonished and didn't want to take it. Father Maximilian literally held
> me and insisted, "You must take it. You're going to do hard labor and
> you're hungry." I took it reluctantly, with sorrow, for I knew he would
> get nothing more until evening.
>
> If I was able to hold out and emerge alive, if I kept my faith and didn't
> fall into despair, I owe it all to Father Maximilian. When I was close to
> despair and ready to throw myself on the wires, he was the one who
> gave me new courage and told me I would be victorious and get out
> alive. "Only keep relying on the intercession of the Mother of God," he
> urged. Somehow he infused in me a strong faith and lively hope, espe-
> cially in her motherly protection. Twice he heard my confession. I go to
> confession frequently, but I often tell my wife that I have never in all my
> life found another confessor so kind as Father Maximilian.
>
> He himself was never discouraged but always the same — friendly,
> open and sincere, and calm.
>
> At this time I was transferred to a squad that worked outside the
> camp with some nonprisoners. I won the trust of some of these people
> and they began giving me things for us prisoners. I smuggled in 400
> Marks and thirty religious medals they gave me, and brought them to
> Father Maximilian. He blessed the medals and distributed them. Truly a
> religious who never forgot his vow of poverty, he divided the money
> among the others, keeping not a single Mark for himself.
>
> Another time a woman got some hosts for me, which I brought in by
> hiding them in a can. I gave them to Father and he celebrated Mass

twice with great secrecy in between the Blocks. About thirty of us attended and received communion from his hands. He could have been punished with death for this.

My friends outside were willing to give foodstuffs as well, but these were more difficult to smuggle past the strict search at the camp gate. I confided to Father Maximilian that, although I would like to bring in food, I was very much afraid of the meticulous inspections. He said, "Put yourself under the protection of the Immaculata. I'll pray. She'll help you." Inspired by the faith he had in Mary's intercession with God, I began. One day I had hidden on me a good-sized loaf of bread and, strapped around my legs, a kilo of lard. Although I was scrupulously searched by the SS man at the gate, somehow he found nothing. I told Father Maximilian, who said, "Trust in the Immaculata and she will help you like this more than once."

I kept on and saved Henry Cyankiewicz and a number of other men from starvation. I brought food to Father Maximilian too. So as not to hurt my feelings, he always took it, but he immediately distributed it to others, keeping nothing for himself.

Francis Mleczko's memories indicate that Kolbe's prayers may have obtained more than just success at passing SS friskings for his fellow prisoners, a hint at why, in spite of the fact they were already imprisoned in 1940 or 1941, so many associated with Father Maximilian are among the 65,000 survivors out of 405,000 on camp rolls (only 5,000 were found alive in the camp itself). Mleczko, who today lives in Webster, Massachusetts, is the man who recalled how the news of Father Kolbe's arrival at Auschwitz went around the death camp. He says:

Like many, I had heard a lot about him before the war. He was famous as the man whose daily newspaper beat out all its competitors. They used to lay traps for him to try and stop him, but he came out of every ambush with more circulation than before. His secret? Ah, that was Maria. I had become a member of his spiritual Militia, but I had seen his bearded face only in photographs. When word circulated that Father Maximilian was in the new transport of prisoners I said to myself, "I want to see him." And I tried to find him, no easy matter since there were twenty-eight Blocks each with six or seven hundred prisoners, all reduced to boney, clean-shaven figures in the same striped pants and top. Even his beard would be gone. It was also dangerous to walk through other Blocks, where you weren't known, asking questions. [Ted Wojtkowski recalls a priest friend, now in Canada, who did, relying on his being a priest to protect him. Believing him a phony, a Nazi plant, other prisoners beat him up.]

After some futile efforts, I abandoned the search. I didn't know that shortly after I gave up, he was moved to my Block so that we were rubbing shoulders every day as we queued up for soup, for work, for the daily counts, that we were sleeping near each other on the floor and perhaps exchanging the nasty vermin who crawled from one sleeping man to another carrying typhus and other diseases.

During this time when he was in my Block, except for a few intimate friends of his, people didn't know who he was. He gave his occupation in such general terms that no one realized this was the famous Maximilian Kolbe of Niepokalanow. And I think that was what he wanted — to become like the rest of us — just another Adam, as we say, an Everyman rather than someone special. What strikes me now is that he was the man who didn't boast.

At this time, every Sunday during the count a list of about twenty consecutive numbers would be read. Then the order would be repeated: "Tomorrow do not report for work. Remain in your Block. At nine o'clock your Block foreman will take you to the kitchen." What this meant was that Monday you would be shot. All of us knew that well because it happened the same way each week. While the rest of the camp was at work, the men whose numbers had been called were ordered to undress. Then they were taken to the execution wall beside Block 11 and shot in the back of the head. We would see their corpses stacked up when we came back. These numbers were following a sequence. They passed 6,000, then 7,000. My number was in the 7,400s. A day came when I figured out I had only a week of life left. Next Sunday would be my last. I wanted to go to confession. Although there were two diocesan priests from Poznan in Block 14, I didn't want to go to them because they were close friends of mine. I told them all this and they said, "That's all right. There's another priest in the Block.". . . Only then did I find out he was Maximilian Kolbe.

He was glad to hear my confession. It was strictly against the rules, of course, so we did it while walking along outside as if we were just talking. When it came time for absolution, he shook my hand. That was the sign we had prearranged. He encouraged me also, but he knew from the way I encouraged others that I was not breaking down. There was nothing dramatic. I think he said he would pray for me, but that would certainly not be unusual under the circumstances.

That was a Friday or a Saturday. The next day, Sunday, I expected my number to come up and to be shot on Monday. Sunday came and they didn't call any numbers. It was like a miracle. And so here I am today still alive. Later they began again but somehow with numbers past mine. And even when they backtracked eventually to pick up the missing ones, these never included mine. I was so heartened! I can only repeat the whole thing was very much like a miracle. And although I said nothing to anyone about my thoughts, interiorly I made some connection between what had happened and Father Maximilian's hearing what I think I explained to him would be my last confession.

In February 1941, after six weeks in Pawiak, Father Sigismund Ruszczak, a younger priest, was shipped to Auschwitz. As a seminarian, he had met Kolbe. Except for Conrad Szweda's, his is the only priest's portrait of Kolbe in Auschwitz:

How great was his immeasurable, marvelous humanity! He was so good. He loved God more than himself. And he loved every man in God. What an apostle! I can't say I made that kind of impression as a priest. I was afraid of suffering. And my desire to live was so intense I was always searching opportunities to eat.

One day I was supporting Father Maximilian under the arm as we walked and talked, when I felt that he stuck a piece of bread in my coat.

"But then you won't have any, Father?" I argued insincerely, for I desperately wanted to eat that bread at once.

"Have it!" he urged. "You're young. You need it more than I!"

"But surely you're hungry, Father?" I protested weakly.

"I'm not hungry," he assured me. "Here, take it."

So I ate greedily. It was really *panis vitae,* the bread of life for me. Once I remember he also gave me some soup.

Although like every other prisoner he wore dirty, torn clothes with a bowl hanging at his side — a worn-out, degraded human skeleton of a man, like the rest — somehow in him all that was obliterated by the charm of his spiritualized countenance and the sanctity radiating from his personality.

I never met him without feeling a real emanation of his goodness and wonderful peace in my soul. I liked to look into his beautiful, deep-set eyes which had such warmth, charm, and sweetness.

In a certain sense the concentration camp was beneficial to me. There was certainly nothing routine about my prayers. Intense, anguished, filled with the deepest faith and salted with tears — that's how I prayed at Auschwitz. When I came in contact with Father Kolbe, I was still reproaching God rebelliously: "Why? Why? How can you permit all this?" At that time Father still bore bruises and signs of beating, but he never complained. It was he who helped me penetrate the meaning of suffering.

I remember a day I met him on the assembly square. I asked him to hear my confession. It was a great thing to me to confide my sins and difficulties to a saint and to receive absolution and comfort from his lips.

My confession ended, he said, "Now I want to go to confession to you." And I heard him. Today I thank God for such graces and that he bequeathed to me an iota of his great spirit.

It can be said there is no Father Kolbe without his love for the Blessed Mother of Christ. But this love of his was sublime, theological, universal. One had to be a kindred spirit, an identical soul to understand him. In this veritable hell of the greatest suffering and cruelty, of satanic degradation, of cursing, and the misery of sin, to me he was like the flash of a brilliant light of God and beauty.

We were talking one Sunday. I asked, "Will we ever leave this place? Be free?"

"You will be free," he said emphatically. "You will live to see freedom." Then he added, "We all have a mission to fulfill — all of us here suffering in this camp. You will get out. I will not because I have a mission — the Immaculata has a mission to fulfill. . . ."

He spoke as always with quiet conviction.

Who was Father Kolbe?

That will remain forever God's deep mystery.

Perhaps one of those "kindred spirits" Father Ruszczak mentions who really understood Kolbe's message is veterinarian Ladislaus Lewkowicz. Lewkowicz knew Father Maximilian prior to Auschwitz, having spent about a year at Niepokalanow—in 1937, at age sixteen—before deciding his vocation was not to religious life. He was twenty to Kolbe's forty-seven in 1941, when they met again in imprisonment.

From the very first day he arrived at the death camp, I often met him following the evening roll call. Although his head was usually bent for-ward — perhaps because of his poor health — and he spoke slowly and low, his words gave me hope and strength to support the camp suffer-ings with great, deep satisfaction and joy. After listening to him, I felt myself no longer afraid to die, a prospect constantly threatening one.

From our conversations I learned that the Germans had pillaged the friary, carried away its printing equipment, and that he had been cruelly beaten in Warsaw; but he did not speak willingly of his sufferings and accepted all this peacefully.

He was assigned to the heaviest labor down by the Sola River. When the capo beat him savagely, I had to learn this from Father Pius [Barto-sik]. I questioned Father Maximilian, pressed him for a reply, and finally he admitted it. I expressed my deep sorrow. He replied that he was glad to suffer; that everything came from the Lord. All one could see in him was peace, humility, total submission to God's will, and great compas-sion for his fellow prisoners.

Until his death he was my confessor. His last fatherly word to me was, "Keep yourself far from even little sins."

Sometimes I wanted to lend him a few pennies so that he could buy a little soup in the canteen, but he wouldn't accept so as not to diminish my money. But he was ready to give anything of his own to others.

We were always angling for easier work. He said, "It's all the same to me; may God's will be done." While the rest of us impatiently looked for liberation, he never said he'd like to go back to Niepokalanow, but instead said he wanted whatever God and the Immaculata wanted. "That will be best." Another trait I noticed was that whereas other priests and Brothers would talk of their hunger and longing for a morsel of bread, in this camp where a piece of bread made the difference between life and death, Father Maximilian simply never mentioned such things. Plunged in God, he lived as though he were in another world.

I inquired a few times into his inner life. It was certainly different from ours. There was in him, I believe, a special grace, for he was always serene, his spirit at peace. He had the gift of prayer. I often saw him walking along, his head bent slightly forward, wrapped in prayer. And since he fulfilled God's will and commandments, he possessed the love of God. In the concentration camp where we were crushed by inhuman sufferings and robbed of faith, he not only accepted everything as from God's hand, but thanked him and loved him all the more.

15

The Last Battle

THE FIRST BIG hurdle was to last for three weeks. Anyone who could do that was said to have a chance to survive for three months. After that the sky was the limit, but not many made it.

Jan Dudzinski's comments are echoed by others. Dysentery from the inadequate diet was a big killer among the inexperienced. How did Kolbe fare? He suffered pneumonia in Pawiak and again at Auschwitz and was beaten a number of times—once almost to death. He worked in two of the hardest work squads under killer capos. Yet he had come out of all of it alive.

A physiologically frail individual whose tuberculosis might be easily reactivated by hard labor, inadequate clothing, and the starvation diet, Kolbe should not have been surviving the way he was. The explanation must be found in his union with God. Research today makes clear that stress and emotions have a great deal to do with who succumbs in such a situation and who does not. Sensitive prisoners, reeling with shock and horror, felt abandoned by God and man. Tougher men blazed with hate. Kolbe, a mystical spouse of Christ whose feminine and masculine elements were so perfectly integrated that Szweda can speak in the same breath of his manly attitude toward suffering and his mother's heart, maintained his serenity.

Imagine what it meant in Auschwitz to be spared the stress of fear, of suicidal depression, of hate. Imagine what it meant not to be driven mad by the question, "Why are they doing this to me?" To find meaning in every suffering, coin with which to purchase great treasures for the ones one loves. Imagine that where everyone else saw himself a squirming victim in the tormentor's hand, Kolbe believed he was a knight on a noble, mystical mission. Those familiar with mystics and saints will also understand why Kolbe could give away part of his starvation rations so frequently without quickly becoming a "Mussulman." Without denying that he sacrificed in doing so and suffered from hunger—perhaps even greatly—it is also true that great mystics can live on amazingly little food as they tap directly into the ultimate source of energy. (Jesus appears to acknowledge this when his disciples were urging him to eat after an unspecified period without food, and he replied, "I have food to eat of which you do not know. . . . Doing the will of Him who sent me and bringing His work to completion is my food" (John 4:31–34).

With these points in mind, it appears less incredible that the physician-prisoner Dr. Francis Wlodarski, who lived with Kolbe in his last Block and, as a friend, spent a lot of time with him, says, "He was in good physical condition" after eight weeks of imprisonment.

Staying in good condition as a *priest*—and therefore subject to some of the worst work details—was no easy task. Few long-term survivors worked in the jobs Kolbe had. The key to survival, says Ted Wojtkowski, was to get a job under a roof. Because of his knowledge of German, Ted, a twenty-one-year-old university student in engineering, got a job as a prisoner foreman in the warehouse that served the Gestapo as a PX. He never went hungry. Jan Dudzinski got into the camp carpenter shop making chairs for the guards after a grueling stint at farm labor, where frostbite (prisoners had only their denim uniform and clogs against the cruel Polish winter) had almost sentenced him to execution. Later, since he knew German, he worked in a printing shop outside the camp where Nazi propaganda posters were produced. In both situations, the work foremen provided their crews with extra food. In the print shop Dudzinski was given so much that he could give his camp rations to hungrier friends.

In theory, even German-speaking priests did not get these good jobs. But in life there are always exceptions. Father Conrad Szweda worked in the hospital. Certainly the brilliant, charismatic Kolbe, fluent in German and several other languages including Russian, with dozens of skills important where there were factories, an intuitive man who knew just how to handle others, a mystic who read hearts, a natural leader who attracted all kinds of people (many of whom wanted to help him), and certainly a masterful tactician, could have parlayed all these assets into a safe voyage through even Auschwitz.

For unless one was taken directly from boxcar to gas chamber, as several million were, survival at Auschwitz, from a human point of view, was not totally a matter of chance but also of skill in avoiding trouble, knowing how to work to keep going, how to eat, and so on. Kolbe's friend Joseph Sobolewski has testified that Kolbe gave others excellent practical advice on such matters. Dudzinski recalls friends who died because they impetuously ate grass raw (instead of salted and cooked),* tried to eat coal because someone said margarine was made from it, or indulged in other reckless measures that a master of self-control like Father Maximilian would never have been guilty of. Ted Wojtkowski used his intuition and cool head to outwit several SS camps until 1945, when he was one of the few survivors of a death march. The intelligent resourcefulness and strong-hearted endurance of Ted Wojtkowski are precisely the qualities Maximilian Kolbe excelled in.

But Kolbe did not survive Auschwitz.

If it was not for lack of resources, it was also not a question of bad luck. He was never condemned. His death was a purely supernatural event. He himself explained it in advance to the young priest Sigismund Ruszczak that summer of 1941. To Ruszczak he said, without giving any further details, that he would not be leaving the camp alive because he had a mission to do for God through the Immaculata. Another priest friend, John Lipski, recalls that Kolbe said to him, "We must do a great work for God here." Lipski adds, "I thought then from his words and expression that

---

*They went "loco" and were murdered by injection immediately.

he had the intention of doing something special in the camp which
would help our fellow prisoners." With his leadership, this might
have meant initiating in the camp the underground resistance begun later by Poles and Austrians. But the man who insisted to
Joseph Stemler that "only love is creative" did not wish to fight the
Nazis but to triumph over them through love. Long ago, in the
vision that called him to sanctity, Mary had held out to him the
mystical white crown reserved for the pure in heart and body. He
had earned it early and re-earned it in Auschwitz. But there had
been a blood-colored crown as well, the one reserved for the man
who overcomes his instinctive clinging to this existence to offer his
very life for another out of love of God. To glorify God who can
forge such heroes and call down the blessings of such a sacrifice on
the camp, Kolbe put on the armor of God (see Ephesians 6:14 and
I Thessalonians 5:8) and, drawing his strength from the Lord's
mighty power (Ephesians 6:10), he waited for this final battle.

On July 24 or 25, after two months in Auschwitz, Kolbe was
transferred from the so-called Invalid's Block (in this place of recu-
peration men were in even greater danger of starvation, because
they got only half-rations) to Block 14. A forty-year-old Polish
army sergeant, Francis Gajowniczek, who had been at the death
camp since September 1940, also lived in Block 14. Tough but
devout, this professional soldier would play a leading part in
Kolbe's final mystical battle although he didn't know Kolbe well.
He says:

> I observed him evenings in the Block praying fervently and inviting
> others to join him — a very dangerous activity. I participated in prayer
> sessions he organized, and once was among his listeners at a confer-
> ence he gave right outside the Block.
>
> Another day a bunch of us were shoveling manure out of a pit. Father
> Kolbe was beaten very cruelly by an SS guard who hit him many times
> in the face while his attack dog also assaulted Father, biting him serious-
> ly. Father Kolbe bore all this not just with patience but with dignity.
> When he returned to the pit where we were throwing out the manure,
> he continued work without a word.
>
> As I saw him around, he seemed a very open and honest person.
> Although he was noticeable for never trying to arrange better condi-
> tions for himself, I recall that when he was put down for a better work

squad — that of washing potatoes in the kitchen — he expressed his happiness openly to us and his gratitude toward God and the intercession of the Virgin Mary.

I also noticed his great compassion toward the "Musselmen," whom he tried to sustain morally and by hearing their confessions in spite of the serious trouble this could have caused him.

Ted Wojtkowski lived upstairs in Block 14 while Kolbe, like Gajowniczek, was on the first floor. Wojtkowski says:

> In this mass of humanity, where almost everyone was a number (because you only got the names of those who maybe slept right next to you or worked with you and so became friends), it was dangerous to get inquisitive or not to mind your own business.

For this reason, he didn't know Kolbe personally. But he remembered later that a couple of his buddies had gone to confession to Father Maximilian. One repeated to Ted the priest's remark: "If I have to die, I would like it to be on the feast of Our Lady."

As July came to an end, the next feast of the Mother of God, that of her assumption into heaven, lay fifteen days away. With harvest season in full swing, one prisoner assigned to swell the farm details began dreaming of escape through the open fields. Joseph Sobolewski, who arrived at Auschwitz in August 1940 as number 2,877 in the first Warsaw transport, recalls that there had already been two prisoners that summer who successfully fled that way. But the Nazis made sure such events were no occasion for rejoicing among those left behind. It took a certain kind of desperation to run away, knowing what others would pay. On almost the last day of July, the dreamer had become that desperate. Francis Mleczko remembers:

> We were working digging gravel (to be used in building more Blocks) outside the camp when suddenly, about three in the afternoon, the sirens began to wail and shriek. That was a terrible sign. It meant there had been an escape. At once the German sentries lifted their guns, counted us, and began to keep an extrastrict watch. Besides scrutinizing our every movement, the guards were also alert for any sign of the escapee who might be hiding, for all they knew, in a field, a tree, on a floor, inside a vehicle, or any one of a thousand places.
>
> The siren's crescendo not only alerted the SS and capos outside the

camp, it even reached the villages outside the fifteen-mile penal zone, warning the police to set up roadblocks and watch for the poor fugitive. The thoughts of all of us were not on him, however, but ourselves; for if the escapee was from our Block, we knew ten to twenty of us would die in reprisal. So I prayed, and I imagine everyone else was doing the same: "Oh please don't let him be from my Block. Let him be from Block 3 or Block 8 but not from 14."

But when we returned to camp, the worst proved true — the missing man was from Block 14.

That evening, according to Pallotine Brother Ladislaus Swies who had joined Kolbe in song in the suffocating boxcar that carried them to Auschwitz:

After work the whole camp stood at attention until we were dismissed to go to bed. No one got even a bite to eat. But the following morning, after just coffee, we had to go to another hard day's work — except for Block 14, which had the missing prisoner. They were again put on the parade ground to stand all day in the sun.*

Ted Wojtkowski was one of the standers on what he recalls as a nice summer day:

We stood at attention in the sun — boiling — from morning until late afternoon, with our only break at noon when we were given our soup ration. Quite a few keeled over and were left lying however they fell.

Maximilian Kolbe, over twice Ted's age, *not* sustained by Nazi warehouse food, and barely recovered from his recent second bout with pneumonia, stood. As the day drew finally to a close, attended by sharp-eyed SS lieutenants and noncoms, Kommandant Höss's deputy-commander Fritsch made his appearance, well-fed and immaculate in his sharply creased uniform and shining jackboots. He faced the quaking rows of dirty, blood-spotted, blue-gray stripes. He would announce to the physically drained and terrified men their fate.

Wojtkowski, Mleczko, Mieczyslaus Koscielniak, Alexsy Kucharski, Francis Gajowniczek, and Francis Wlodarski were all

---

*Most survivors participated in a number of such line-ups, which memory has tended to blur together. Some Block 14 survivors believe that on this occasion there was no day of standing before the reprisal.

among the six hundred men of Block 14 who, with Kolbe, formed ten lines of approximately sixty men each, these in graduated ranks by height from the shortest prisoners in front to the tallest in back. Dr. Wlodarski was about three places away from Father Maximilian. Joseph Sobolewski, lawyer and military man, who used to talk with his friends about Kolbe's gift of reading their hearts, was in the last row of the adjoining Block and could see perfectly the drama about to unfold. The tailor Alexander Dziuba also had a good view, although from his testimony it is unclear whether he was in or out of Block 14 itself. Another friend of Kolbe's, George Bielecki, the technician, was watching from a window. Brother Ladislaus Swies was on the parade ground about fifteen meters away from Fritsch, with a good view. All these men have given accounts of what was about to occur. Some saw and engraved on their memory almost everything. Others remember only one or two striking details. A few heard what was said. Others deduced from gestures or a word or two. Rather than switch back and forth from witness to witness, since accounts vary only in small particulars such as phrasing, the following account is composed of the men's combined memories. To give some idea of the intense self-absorption of the average man whose life is at stake, Mleczko's and Wojtkowski's memories are inserted. They show vividly what was going on in the minds of 599 men. The inner state of Maximilian Kolbe, whether exaltation, dread, or resolution, can only be pondered.

Germans are celebrated as masters of detail and lovers of order, good qualities that in Auschwitz were put to evil use. With the ranks arranged by height, the dapper Fritsch could efficiently scan many of the emaciated faces. As he looked them over, they all seemed to cease to breathe. The silence was absolute.

At this moment, Wojtkowski is keyed up, hoping desperately he has successfully hidden in almost, but not exactly, the middle of a sixty-man row and, in spite of his height, not in the ninth or tenth row where a man stands out, but in the eighth row. He hopes fervently that by the time Fritsch reaches the eighth row the number of victims will have been selected. If not, with only one or two to be chosen, hopefully the sub-führer will skip the eighth row to go onto the final lines. This is the best strategy the resourceful Wojtkowski can come up with. He can only hope it will work.

Breathless, in about the fifth row near one end, Francis Mleczko is thinking of his family and praying.

To the assembled, fear-stricken eyes looking directly at him because they have no choice, Fritsch barks, "The fugitive has not been found. In reprisal for your comrade's escape, ten of you will die by starvation. Next time, it will be twenty." Immediately the selection begins. Palitsch and a prisoner-secretary precede him with pad and pencil to take down the numbers of the condemned; Fritsch walks down the first row of identically garbed, nameless men. He meanders slowly to prolong their terror. Perhaps he is even so sick that he enjoys the feeling that each life is momentarily his to dangle helplessly before its owner before setting it down or shattering it forever. He scrutinizes faces. Then, with a gesture, he chooses his first victim from the front row. This does not mean the rest in that line are safe, however. He might take another. Even when the tenth man is chosen, the SS had been known to go on and take eleven, twelve, thirteen—as many as eighteen. After the first row is inspected, the order is given: "Three paces forward." They move up, leaving an alley between them and the second row so the arrogant Fritsch can one by one, stare each of these hapless souls straight in the face, while musing with leisurely care on his fate. Francis Mleczko recalls:

> I was in about the fifth or sixth row back and the fifth or sixth man from the end Fritsch started at. As he came closer and closer my heart was pounding. "Let him pass me, let him pass me, oh pass, pass," I was praying. But no. He stopped directly before me. With his eyes, he examined me from my head to my feet, then back again. A second complete up and down. I saw the [secretary] pose his pencil to write my number. Then, in Polish, Fritsch orders, "Open your mouth." I open. He looks. He walks on. I breathe again.

They are coming to Kolbe. His admirers can only think God will never permit a son who has given his whole life to his Father's work—and whose work of studding the world with Christian communication centers is so far from finished—to be condemned by these agents of evil. Right. Fritsch does not even pause.

But now he is beckoning to Palitsch. They are examining Koscielniak, who watches the two SS officers exchange looks:

> It seemed to me this look would never end and in a moment I would

be called out. . . . But no, they passed me and chose someone else. I
began to tremble from relief. . . .

The line of the forlorn souls, the condemned, is growing. At each
selection, Fritsch's newest victim steps out forever from the Block
ranks to join this death row. When the SS officer reaches the
eighth row, the sinister quota is almost filled. Wojtkowski:

> I am thinking my luck is okay. Then suddenly he points down the row
> at me and calls "You!" I freeze in terror and can't move. Since I don't
> put my foot forward, my neighbor decides Fritsch is calling him. Unsure,
> he puts one foot slightly out.
>
> "Not you, dummkopf Polish swine," Fritsch snarls, and points at me
> again. Then suddenly, in a split second, he changes his mind and, as my
> neighbor starts to step back, he orders him forward and takes him in-
> stead of me. I remain paralyzed. . . .

Finally the grisly selection is complete. Fritsch turns to Palitsch,
the noncommissioned officer who likes to brag about the numbers
he has shot at the execution wall by Block 11. Together the SS
officers check the secretary's list against the numbers on the condemned. As their German passion for accuracy occupies them, one
of the victims is sobbing, "My wife and my children!" It is Francis
Gajowniczek. The SS ignore him.

Suddenly, there is movement in the still ranks. A prisoner several rows back has broken out and is pushing his way toward the
front. The SS guards watching this Block raise their automatic
rifles, while the dogs at their heels tense for the order to spring.
Fritsch and Palitsch too reach toward their holsters. The prisoner
steps past the first row.

It is Kolbe. His step is firm, his face peaceful. Angrily, the Block
capo shouts at him to stop or be shot. Kolbe answers calmly, "I
want to talk to the commander," and keeps on walking while the
capo, oddly enough, neither shoots nor clubs him. Then, still at a
respectful distance, Kolbe stops, his cap in his hands. Standing at
attention like an officer of some sort himself, he looks Fritsch
straight in the eye.

"Herr Kommandant, I wish to make a request, please," he says
politely in flawless German.

Survivors will later say it is a miracle that no one shoots him.
Instead, Fritsch asks, "What do you want?"

"I want to die in place of this prisoner," and Kolbe points toward the sobbing Gajowniczek. He presents this audacious request without a stammer. Fritsch looks stupefied, irritated. Everyone notes how the German lord of life and death, suddenly nervous, actually steps back a pace.

The prisoner explains coolly, as if they were discussing some everyday matter, that the man over there has a family.

"I have no wife or children. Besides, I'm old and not good for anything. He's in better condition," he adds, adroitly playing on the Nazi line that only the fit should live.

"Who are you?" Fritsch croaks.

"A Catholic priest."

Fritsch is silent. The stunned Block, audience to this drama, expect him in usual Auschwitz fashion to show no mercy but sneer, "Well, since you're so eager, we'll just let you come along too," and take both men. Instead, after a moment, the deputy-commander snaps, "Request granted." As if he needs to expel some fury, he kicks Gajowniczek, snarling, "Back to ranks, you!"

Prisoners in ranks are never allowed to speak. Gajowniczek says:

> I could only try to thank him with my eyes. I was stunned and could hardly grasp what was going on. The immensity of it: I, the condemned, am to live and someone else willingly and voluntarily offers his life for me – a stranger. Is this some dream or reality? . . .

Now the order is given for the condemned to march and then the Block is dismissed. Brother Ladislaus says:

> The ten victims walked in front of me and I saw that Father Kolbe was staggering under the weight of one of the others as he upheld this man who could not walk with his own strength.

Some of his buddies rush over to Ted Wotjkowski, who is still dazed, benumbed by his own near death-sentence and by the sacrifice he has just seen. "C'mon, let's forget it," they urge, but Ted stands there as if paralyzed still. He is thinking, "I've just seen a saint made."

16

The Tabernacle

T HE HEART OF every Catholic institution is the chapel with its
tabernacle housing the living God. From there, believers
feel powerful, sweet radiations.

Auschwitz, too, had a spiritual heart from which radiated agony,
despair, and death. This was the prison within the prison, the penal Block called the bunker, where in the basement the SS "interrogated" prisoners with unspeakable cruelty. In one of these cells,
made airtight for the occasion, the first gassings would be done on
hapless hospital patients, Jews and Russian prisoners of war.

It was here Kolbe entered like a sliver of light into a black pit.
He who without prudery was so modest was naked. The SS guard
had snarled, "Strip," while they were still outside the Block. No
sense in his having to carry their garments up the stairs. Then it
was in the door of the innocent-looking brick building and descent
into the dark, fetid basement where they were shoved into one of
the rank-smelling cells.

"You'll dry up like tulips," their jailer sneered as he slammed
the door.

How do we know? Former SS men do not exactly come forward
in droves to testify to their heartlessness. Their victims are dead.

There were, however, prisoner secretary-interpreters even in this infamous Block 11. To ensure their silence on what went on there, these men were liquidated from time to time like the later crematorium workers.

By some act of God, the prisoner-interpreter who would watch Kolbe's last days came out of Auschwitz alive. Number 1,192, Bruno Borgowiec was a Pole from Silesia, the rich, coal-mining region whose ownership has changed hands among several countries, including Germany and Poland. He worked with the other earliest prisoners building the camp; then, because of his perfect German, he was given the very dangerous job of interpreter in the penal Block. One can only imagine the things he was forced to see, to hear. Suffice it to say Bruno Borgowiec died on the Monday after Easter in 1947, when he was only about forty years old. But not before he had written Niepokalanow on December 27, 1945, with many details of what he had seen and left two notarized, sworn statements, one brief, the other more detailed, of the last days of the man he considered "a hero and a saint."

It is Borgowiec who provides the details of what those who know Kolbe would suspect: The starvation cell, far from defeating him, would become a tabernacle in this cruelest part of Auschwitz, as if—hidden in the heart of the humble Franciscan—God had snuck into Hell.

Borgowiec explains why he could repeat even the SS man's cruel jest as he locked the victims into their death cell, where only a tiny window high up against the basement ceiling let in a little light. In spite of thousands having died in that bunker, he remembered even such isolated details about Father Kolbe's last days "with absolute clarity," he maintained, "because of the absolutely extraordinary behavior with which the noble Father faced death." I combine Borgowiec's various reports:

> The naked victims were in one cell near those [dying in reprisal because] of the two previous escapes. The foul air was horrible, the cell floor cement. There was no furniture whatsoever, except for a bucket for relieving themselves.
>
> You could say Father Kolbe's presence in the bunker was necessary for the others. They were in a frenzy over the thoughts of never returning to their homes and families, screaming in despair and cursing. He pacified them and they [began to] resign themselves. With his gift of

consolation, he prolonged the lives of the condemned who were usually so psychologically destroyed that they succumbed in just a few days.

To keep up their spirits, he encouraged them that the escapee might still be found and they would be released.* [Koscielniak talked to the German Streiberg and the bunker chief, who told him Kolbe was hearing the victims' confessions and preparing them to die.] So they could join him, he prayed aloud. The cell doors were made of oak. Because of the silence and acoustics, the voice of Father Kolbe in prayer was diffused to the other cells, where it could be heard well. These prisoners joined in.

From then on, every day from the cell where these poor souls were joined by the adjoining cells, one heard the recitation of prayers, the rosary, and hymns. Father Kolbe led while the others responded as a group. As these fervent prayers and hymns resounded in all corners of the bunker, I had the impression I was in a church.

Outside the penal Block, Francis Mleczko recalls that the prisoners were keeping a kind of prayer vigil in their free hours, walking past the tiny window where only the top of a head could be seen. Szweda had even rashly gone to the death Block to inquire. He was growled at by a prisoner who worked there, "You fool, don't you know better than to ask questions like that? Do you want to end up here too? Run away fast before someone sees you."

Borgowiec continues:

> Once a day the SS men in charge of the penal Block inspected the cells, ordering me to carry away the corpses of those who had died during the night. I also always had to be present for these inspections because, as secretary-interpreter, it was my job to write down the numbers of the dead and also to translate from Polish into German any conversation or questions asked by the condemned.
>
> Sometimes Father Kolbe's group was so deeply absorbed in prayer that they didn't notice the SS opening the door. It took loud shouts to get their attention. When they saw the cell door was opened, the poor wretches, weeping, would loudly beg for a crust of bread and some water, which they never obtained. If one of those who still had the strength approached the door, right away the SS would kick the poor

---

* Actually, according to all the survivors, even if a prisoner were found, no condemned were ever reprieved.

man in the stomach so [hard] that falling back on the cement floor he would die or, if not, they would shoot him.*

Father Kolbe never asked for anything and he never complained.

He looked directly and intently into the eyes of those entering the cell. Those eyes of his were always strangely penetrating. The SS men couldn't stand his glance, and used to yell at him, "Schau auf die Erde, nicht auf uns!" ("Look at the ground, not at us.")

Physician Francis Wlodarski was also told by a Nazi patient, the penal bunker chief, with whom he maintained good relations in order to get news, that Kolbe was "a psychic trauma, a shock" for the SS men who had to bear his look—a look that hungered (not that the penal chief put it this way) not for bread but to liberate them from evil. This Nazi's evaluation of Kolbe: "An extremely courageous man, really a superhuman hero." Borgowiec continues:

I overheard the SS talking about him among themselves. They were admiring his courage and behavior. One of them said, "So einen wie diesen Pfarrer haben wir hier noch nicht gehabt. Das muss ein ganz aussergewöhnlicher Mensch sein." ("We've never had a priest here like this one. He must be a wholly exceptional man.")

While the SS men were absent, I used to go down and console my countrymen. [Through the keyhole or the hinged observation window, Borgowiec also passed Kolbe's group vitamin C, which he got from friends in the hospital; after awhile he desisted, realizing that if he were extending their lives, he was only prolonging their agony.]

What kind of martyrdom these men were enduring can be imagined from the fact that the urine bucket was always dry. In their dreadful thirst, they must have drunk its contents.

As the prisoners became weaker, the prayers continued, but in whispers. But even when during each inspection the others were always found lying on the cement, Father Kolbe was still standing or kneeling, his face serene.

In this way, two weeks went by. The prisoners were dying one after the other, and by this time only four were left, among them Father Kolbe, who was still conscious. The SS decided things were taking too long. . . . One day they sent for the German criminal Bock from the

---

* It is unclear from Borgowiec's comments, which were translated from Italian, whether he is speaking generally or of prisoners from Kolbe's specific group.

hospital to give the prisoners injections of carbolic acid. After the needle prick in the vein of the left arm, you could follow the instant swelling as it moved up the arm toward the chest. When it reached the heart, the victim would fall dead. Between injection and death was a little more than ten seconds.

When Bock got there, I had to accompany them to the cell. I saw Father Kolbe, with a prayer, himself hold out his arm to the executioner. I couldn't bear it. With the excuse that I had some work to do, I left. But as soon as the SS and their executioner were gone, I returned.

The other naked, begrimed corpses were lying on the floor, their faces betraying signs of their sufferings. Father Kolbe was sitting upright, leaning against the far wall. His body was not dirty like the others, but clean and bright. The head was tilted somewhat to one side. His eyes were open. Serene and pure, his face was radiant.

Anybody would have noticed and thought this was some saint.

Some of Kolbe's friends were brash enough to request that his body not be burned, but buried. The request was denied. Kolbe would not have liked being singled out that way. Years earlier he had said, "I would like to be ground to dust for the Immaculate Virgin and have this dust be blown away by the wind all over the world."

Szweda recalls:

The bodies were to be carried to the crematorium on the morning of August fifteenth. Very devout friends of mine were the ones who had to carry them out in the trough-like wooden boxes. They told me, "Watch closely, the first one we carry out will be Father Maximilian."

I stood watching. As they passed, I took off my striped prisoner's cap, although this was forbidden. Nobody noticed. I was pretty well hidden. I had to watch him like that going to the crematorium. . . .

It is quite common for individuals to die on milestone dates such as a birthday or the anniversary of a spouse's death. Kolbe had said he would like to die on the feast of Our Lady. Fittingly, he was murdered on the vigil of the Assumption of Mary, that is, the evening before the feast. Since the date of a martyr's death, his birthday into heaven, is the date the Church celebrates, those with a sentimental bent will believe that Our Lady had seen to it that her knight's feast would nestle next to her own.

On the July evening when Kolbe stepped boldly through the

ranks to offer his life for a man crying out in anguish, Ted Wojt-kowski had recognized an authentic Christian martyr in the quiet little priest from his Block. But as he tried to stammer out this impression to a friend who now lives in New York, his buddy made a gesture of annoyance, "Aw, come off it, Ted. That was a Musselman. He was fed up."

But this reaction was not the most common. More so was the response of Alexsy Kucharski who, in the front row, saw and heard everything. Kucharski, who today lives in Palm Springs, California, says:

> I was mostly concerned with the fact of my own survival, but I was still extremely moved by Father Kolbe's act.

Kolbe's close friend Mieczyslaus Koscielniak, the artist, explains:

> We were so amazed that we were incapable for the moment of reacting or grasping what had happened. All we could do was to rejoice to our depths that we were not among the doomed. Thank God it isn't me but somebody else that was chosen! Callous as it sounds, that was our first human response.

It was only after the shock of their own survival faded that the realization of Kolbe's sacrifice could begin to swell. His friends mourned, "Our little Father. Not our little Father." At the same time they were proud. Part of Hitler's strategy, based on his pathological hatred of Slavs, was to demean the prisoners—to make them *feel* as subhuman as he claimed they were. Suddenly a Pole had refused to play the role, had given Hitler's supermen a lesson in courage. A "dummkopf,"—"Polnisches Schwein," as Fritsch called them—had made the deputy commander step back in something like awe or fear. Szweda says:

> It was on everybody's lips, though, not just Poles. Czechs, Austrians, people of all nationalities – even the Germans – were dumbfounded and exclaimed, "This is genuine love of neighbor!" because no one had ever volunteered to die before. On the contrary, everyone held onto life to its last threads – and here Father Maximilian gave away, not a piece of his bread or even all his soup, but his very life for another.
>
> And such a death. In starvation like that one has to give oneself up bit by bit, web by web, knowing for sure that one is perishing. . . . To do it

and not break down completely. Some went insane. Or in their animal hunger they attacked the others. Once two men were carried out who had bitten each other to death. But like Father Maximilian to have the presence of mind and will to drink to the very end the chalice of bitterness, contempt and suffering: That is heroism.

Echoing the younger priest's admiration were remarks by Koscielniak, Wojtkowski, Sobolewski, Dziuba, and Wlodarski:

"The death of a martyr and hero."

"A man in need cried out as a human being and found a human being who responded."

"Where everyone thought only of saving his life, he gave his for a stranger."

"This deed was the summit of his love for his fellow man."

"An act of supreme heroism without any imprudence or thoughtlessness about it . . . based purely on supernatural motives because Father Maximilian was in good physical shape, had a lot of people devoted to him and might have held out to leave the camp alive."

"No similar event ever took place at Auschwitz before or after, nor did I ever hear of anything like it in the other concentration camps. He was the only one among us capable of such a heroic deed."

Finally, George Bielecki, speaking for the rest:

It was an enormous shock to the whole camp. We became aware someone among us in this spiritual dark night of the soul was raising the standard of love on high. Someone unknown, like everyone else, tortured and bereft of name and social standing, went to a horrible death for the sake of someone not even related to him. Therefore it is not true, we cried, that humanity is cast down and trampled in the mud, overcome by oppressors, and overwhelmed by hopelessness. Thousands of prisoners were convinced the true world continued to exist and that our torturers would not be able to destroy it. More than one individual began to look within himself for this real world, found it, and shared it with his camp companion, strengthening both in this encounter with evil. To say that Father Kolbe died for one of us or for that person's family is too great a simplification. His death was the salvation of thousands. And on this, I would say, rests the greatness of that death. That's how we felt about it. And as long as we live, we who were at Auschwitz will bow our heads in memory of it as at that time we bowed our heads before the bunker of death by starvation. That was a shock full of optimism, regenerating and giving strength; we were stunned by his act, which became for us a mighty explosion of light in the dark camp night. . . .

Epilogue

TRANSFERRED PRISONERS carried the story to other camps. The outside world read hints in the carefully cryptic letters prisoners such as Brother Ferdinandus Kasz in Dachau were allowed to send from time to time. Auschwitz survivors completed the account in 1945. The Poland that had known Kolbe for his Militia, his publications, and his quiet, joy-filled holiness even during the war began whispering about him as a hero as well.

Among the listeners during the Occupation was young Karol Wojtyla in Cracow. Supporting himself by working in a stone quarry, Wojtyla continued his secret studies for the priesthood, acted in secret patriotic plays, and wrote poetry in his spare time. As the Nazis began their genocidal gassings of Jews, he also helped these hunted Poles escape. One of the lucky ones at that sort of thing, he was never caught, never endured a concentration camp.

For Wojtyla, so different in temperament but sharing so many of the same concerns, Maximilian Kolbe became a spiritual companion and mentor. After the war, when the former laborer soon went from parish priest to bishop and then cardinal, he began pushing for Kolbe's beatification. In this attempt he joined an older priest who had been very active in the Resistance, Poland's much better known postwar senior Cardinal, the Archbishop of Warsaw, Stefan Wyszynski.

Tribunals to receive information on Kolbe were set up in Padua, Warsaw, Cracow, and Nagasaki. Among the hundreds of oral testimonies it seemed odd that so many who had known Maximilian Kolbe in Auschwitz in 1941 had managed to be among the handful who survived to 1945. It seemed less odd to some of the survivors. Alexander Dziuba and Henry Sienkiewicz claimed they were alive because they had begged their dead friend to intercede for them when dangers threatened. Francis Gajowniczek, one of fewer than twenty-five of five hundred to survive a death march in the war's last days, testified to "miraculous escapes" and credited Kolbe's intercession with his overcoming advanced tuberculosis of the spine without an operation. Because he believed that God kept him alive to testify to the world about Kolbe, Gajowniczek would travel to many lands to tell others about the man who died for him.

In spite of his age (he was in his early fifties), Kolbe's old friend Bronislaus Stryczny had emerged alive from Dachau. Although he could not make the trip from the United States, where he was stationed, to testify, he made known what he believed Kolbe had done for him in Dachau. He had contracted gangrene in the camp and his leg was to have been amputated. Since cripples were routinely gassed, he begged Kolbe and another dead friend to intercede for him. The gangrene went away.

Then there was the testimony of Kolbe's friend Paul Takashi, professor of medicine at the University of Nagasaki. Injured when the atomic bomb exploded in 1945, he was taken to a hospital, hemorrhaging to death. Knowing as a physician that he was dying, he invoked Kolbe's help just before slipping into unconsciousness. He awoke to find that, although his fellow doctors had remained helpless to staunch the flow of blood, it had suddenly ceased.

Such testimonies encouraged others to ask Kolbe's intercession. Niepokalanow's archives were soon bulging with letters from those who believed the dead priest had obtained spiritual or material favors for them from God. The Brothers were not surprised. Kolbe had often told them, "In this life, we can only work for God with one hand, because we need to hold on with the other lest we fall ourselves; how wonderful it will be after death, when we can work with both hands!"

The Church Process, however, looks not for miracles but for heroic virtues. In Kolbe's life these were so abundant that it was decided to honor the Franciscan as a confessor—that is, as one who shows Christ to the world by his life—rather than as a martyr, one who witnesses by his death. After that—as signs that the confessor's Cause was not just of men but also of God—two miracles were authenticated on the basis of exhaustive inquiry by medical men as "instantaneous, complete, permanent, and humanly inexplicable cures." (Had Pope Paul chosen to honor Kolbe as a martyr, such signs would have been unnecessary, martyrdom itself being considered a sign.)

Elated Cardinals Wyszynski and Wojtyla led the Polish pilgrims to Beatification ceremonies in Saint Peter's on October 17, 1971. Among the forty-four cardinals, five patriarchs, and approximately three hundred bishops participating were many of the German hierarchy who had joined the Poles in petitioning for Kolbe's recognition as a saint. In a delegation of former death camp inmates was Gajowniczek, who led the offertory procession during the Mass. As Pope Paul VI accepted the ciborium, he embraced the white-haired, seventy-year-old Auschwitz survivor, who wept openly.

From Niepokalanow, Japan, and elsewhere came groups of Franciscan Brothers, priests, members of Kolbe's Militia, and other friends of "our little Father." Everyone pointed out Brother Zeno Zebrowski, his red beard now white, who had sailed with Kolbe to Japan over forty years before. To his intense embarrassment, in Rome as in Japan Brother Zeno was revered and harassed as a living saint.

To all these pilgrims Cardinal Wyszynski said, "Whereas people trust in material resources like tanks, planes, and armies, . . . [Kolbe shows] that only one thing is necessary to gain peace and unity for the world, . . . the practice of love. And that is why Father Maximilian won [his victory] not only on a personal basis, but also on a universal one."

Back in Poland Wyszynski and Wojtyla, joined by Cardinals Krol and Wright of the United States, went to Auschwitz for a triumphal celebration of Kolbe's victory right in Hitler's citadel of hate. Mass was said on a wooden dais inside the ten-foot barbed wire fences on which Dziuba and others had once tried to end their lives in despair. A crowd of 100,000 stretched for more than a mile along the railway bed over which Kolbe had been carried, singing, to imprisonment. To honor the saint, they had come in spite of cold, drizzling rain.

Kolbe had said that Poland must be purified through a period of suffering and then let her light shine on the world. Following the war, even under rule of the Communists, who once again forbade Niepokalanow to publish and who imprisoned the fearless Wyszynski from 1953 to 1956, Poland became a symbol to the world of unquenchable Catholic Christianity. Then in 1978 Wojtyla was elected Pope.

On June 7, 1979, during a tour of his native land, he made a pilgrimage to Auschwitz to lay flowers and pray, kneeling, on the cold cement floor of Kolbe's death cell. To the thousands of Polish faithful who accompanied him, he said simply, "As many times as I have come here, it was impossible for me not to return as Pope." Mourning all those who perished at "this Golgotha of the modern world," particularly the Jews, the pontiff also rejoiced—that in a place "built for the negation of faith . . . and to trample radically not only on love but on all signs of human dignity," Kolbe had won "a victory like that of Christ himself" through "faith and love," while the extermination camp, by that victory, became not just a monument to hate but "a special shrine, the birthplace, I can say, of the patron of our difficult century." On another occasion he remarked that Kolbe had won "the most arduous of victories, that of love which forgives."

The following year the Pope concelebrated Mass with ninety-six priests and two Polish bishops, all Dachau survivors. His face full of emotion, John Paul II told them, "May God repay you for your sufferings, for your sacrifice, and for your witness."

It is rare for a Process to move so fast that canonization takes place while an individual's generation still lives. Because the Pope felt that "this difficult century," buffeted by wars, terrorism, and genocidal hatreds, desperately needed Kolbe as an example and intercessor, Father Maximilian became one of those exceptions.

On October 10, 1982, in the city where he used to serve the Mass of an older priest who still remembers him as "a nice kid," the exuberant Franciscan who wanted to pass God's love on to the whole world was formally enrolled as Saint Maximilian Kolbe by the first Polish Pope. Gajowniczek was in Saint Peter's, as were

Conventual and other Franciscans, Militia members, and Poles from around the world. Represented also were Marytowns in the United States and Brazil and a new institute for women called Missionaries of the Immaculata of Father Kolbe. Brother Zeno and Cardinal Wyszynski were absent, Zeno having died at ninety-one on April 24, the great Cardinal on May 28, a few months short of his eightieth birthday.

Maximilian Kolbe had prayed that he might love everyone "without limits," and confided to physician Rudolph Dien in Auschwitz that he had consecrated his life to "doing good to all men."

In canonizing him, the Church proclaimed that he had succeeded heroically in living those ideals. The Church also extended them beyond the time/space limits of Kolbe's lifetime so that, even when all those who laughed at his jokes at Niepokalanow, tried to follow him to holiness in Japan, or found comfort against his emaciated chest in Auschwitz are dead, new men and women will affirm with death camp survivor Francis Wlodarski, "Because we knew Maximilian Kolbe, we are better human beings."

Sources

LISTED BELOW ARE the "witnesses" included in this book, followed by the sources of each individual's testimony. Where more than one source is cited, the first given is the primary one. This most frequently is *Patavina Seu Cracovien. Beatificationis et Canonizationis Servi Dei Maximiliani M. Kolbe, Sacerdotis Professi Ordinis Fratrum Minor Conventualium.* References to testimonies and depositions included in this 940-page portion of the total Beatification Process materials are cited simply as *Process.* Other sources are listed in full in the first reference; thereafter, citations are greatly abbreviated, usually by author alone.

Achtelik, Brother Ivo, O.F.M. Conv. In Brother Juventyn Mlodozeniec's *I Knew Blessed Maximilian: The Life, Death and Glory of Blessed Maximilian, O.F.M. Conv. (1894–1941).* Translated from the Polish by Sister Mary Consuela Kulikowska, C.S.S.F. Revised edition. Washington, N.J.: AMI Press, 1979, p. 51.

Arzili, Father Alberto. In Maria Winowska's *The Death Camp Proved Him Real.* Translated from the French by Jacqueline Bowers and Father Bernard M. Geiger, O.F.M. Conv. Kenosha, Wis.: PROW, 1971, pp. 57–58. Earliest English edition under the title *Our Lady's Fool,* The Newman Press, 1952. Original French edition (*Le Fou de Notre-Dame: Le Père M. Kolbe*), 1950.

Letter dated April 26, 1942. Translated by Father Bernard M. Geiger, O.F.M. Conv. Reprinted from *Immaculata,* December 1970.

Bielecki, George. *Process.*

Blaszcyk, Brother Vladimir, O.F.M. Conv. In Father Antonio Ricciardi's *Beato Massimiliano Maria Kolbe,* Rome, 1971, p. 296.

Borgowiec, Bruno. *Process.*

Deposition dated October 13, 1946. Translated from the Polish by Father Dominic Wisz, O.F.M. Conv.

Borodziej, Brother Henry, O.F.M. Conv. In "Documents and Witnesses Speak of Father Maximilian Maria Kolbe." Vatican Radio Broadcast. Edited by Andrew Solka. Translated from the Polish by Sister Mary Leocadia, S.S.N.D.*

Buddhist (Paul Miki Koya Tagita). *Process.*

Burdyszek, Father John, O.F.M. Conv. *Father Maximilian Kolbe, O.F.M. Conv.: Fire Enkindled.* Dublin: Clonmore & Reynolds Ltd., 1954.

Chroscicki, Thaddeus L. *Process.*

Cicchito, Father Leon, O.F.M. Conv. In Winowska, pp. 52–53.

Cyankiewicz, Joseph. *Process.*

Czupryk, Father Cornel, O.F.M. Conv. *Process.*

Vatican Radio Broadcast.

Czwojdzinski, Jan. In Mlodozeniec, p. 51.

Dagis, John. Interviews by author April 5 and April 12, 1982, and by phone July 31.

Correspondence with the author dated May 10 and July 28, 1982.

Diem, Rudolph, M.D. *Process.*

Vatican Radio Broadcast.

Drucki-Lubecki, Prince John. *Process.*

Dubianowski, Ladislaus. *Process.*

Dudzinski, Jan. As told to P.J.A. Kennedy. "I Was in Auschwitz with a Saint." *Friar,* September 1972. Reprinted in *Immaculata,* March 1973.

---

*Portions have appeared in publications of the Conventual Franciscans, Marytown, Libertyville, Ill., who made the material available for my use.

Dulude, Brother Camillus, O.F.M. Conv. Interview by the author April 17, 1982, Marytown, Libertyville, Ill.

Dziuba, Alexander. *Process.*

Eccher, Father Andreas, O.F.M. Conv. *Process.*

"Faithless" Japanese (Francis Xavier Hara Susumu). *Process.*

Frejlich, Father Stanley, O.F.M. Conv. Interview (taped) by Brother Francis Mary Kalvelage, O.F.M. Conv., December 1980, Marytown, Libertyville, Ill. Portions published in *Immaculata,* February 1981.

Fukahori, Jacob Yasuro, M.D. *Process.*

Gajowniczek, Francis. *Process.*
Deposition dated November 25, 1946. Translated from the Polish by Father Dominic Wisz, O.F.M. Conv.

Galert, Anna Kolbe. *Process.*

Gastfriend, Eddie. In Tom Fox's "The Survivors: A Message from Auschwitz." *Philadelphia Daily News,* October 10, 1972.

Gibas, Anna Wojtaniowa. *Process.*

Giusta, Father Francesco, O.F.M. Conv. In Ricciardi, p. 304.
Process.

Gniadek, Edward. *Process.*

Gorson, Sigmund. Interview by the author August 8, 1982.

Grodzki, Brother Cyprian, O.F.M. Conv. *Process.*
In Mlodozeniec, p. 62.

Hayasaka, Bishop (of Nagasaki) Januarius Kyunosuke. *Process.*

Ignudi, Father Stephen, O.F.M. Conv. *Log* of Collegio Serafico Internazionale dei Frati Minori Conventuali (The International College of the Friars Minor Conventuals, called the "Seraficum" or "Seraphic College"), Rome.

Juraszek, Brother (no last name given), O.F.M. Conv. In Winowska, pp. 151–152.

Kalucki, Brother Bartholomew (Bart), O.F.M. Conv. Interview (taped) by author through Brother Francis Mary Kalvelage, O.F.M. Conv., May 1982, Milwaukee.

Kasz, Brother Ferdinandus, O.F.M. Conv. *Process.*

Kierszka, Francesca. In Mlodozeniec, p. 55.

Kita, Father Cyril, O.F.M. Conv. *Process.*

Kobla, Rosalia. *Process.*

Koscielniak, Mieczyslaus. *Process.*
Vatican Radio Broadcast.

Kowalska, Janina. *Process.*

Kozbial, Father Isidore, O.F.M., Conv. *Process.*

Koziura, Father Florian, O.F.M. Conv. *Process.*

Kubit, Father Anselm, O.F.M. Conv. *Process.*
Vatican Radio Broadcast.

Kucharski, Alexsy. Correspondence with the author dated May 17, 1982, and June (no day) 1982. Kucharski's eyewitness account of Kolbe's offering his life in Auschwitz was also supplied to the author in an Italian translation from *Miles Immaculatae,* September 1973, by Father Giorgio Domanski, Rome.

Kuszba, Brother Luke, O.F.M. Conv. In Ricciardi, p. 272.
Process.

Langer, Francis. *Process.*

Lebner, Anna. In Mlodozeniec, p. 42.

Lewkowicz, Ladislaus. *Process.*

Lipski, Father John. *Process.*

Maj, Brother Thaddeus, O.F.M. Conv. *Process.*

Majdan, Brother Rufinus, O.F.M. Conv. *Process.*
In Diana Dewars's *Saint of Auschwitz.* London: Darton, Longman & Todd, 1982.

Mleczko, Francis. Interview (taped) by Father James McCurry, O.F.M. Conv., April 3, 1982, and interview (partially taped) by Father McCurry, with questions supplied by the author, June 2, 1982.

Correspondence with the author dated May 29, 1982.

Mlodozeniec, Brother Juventyn, O.F.M. Conv. *I Knew Blessed Maximilian. See* Achtelik, Ivo.

"Father Kolbe's Last Days." *Immaculata Reprints Library,* August 1978.

Correspondence with the author dated May 25, 1982, and August 3, 1982.

Mulzer, Lieutenant Hans. In Mlodozeniec, pp. 43–47.

Nazim, Father Justin, O.F.M. Conv. *Process.*

Obidzinski, Father Vladimir. *Process.*

Orlini, Father Alphonse, O.F.M. Conv. *Process.*

Pal, Father Joseph Peter, O.F.M. Conv. *Process.*

In Winowska, p. 58.

Excerpt from "Minute Books" of Militia Immaculata headquarters, Rome. Translated by Father Bernard M. Geiger, O.F.M. Conv. *Immaculata Reprints Library,* no date given.

Pesiek, Brother Sergius, O.F.M. Conv. Anonymous account attributed to the Brother himself describing Kolbe and the Japanese Mission, based on the author's diary, first-hand reports by fellow Brothers—especially Brother Zeno—and six hundred letters written by Kolbe between 1930 and 1936.

Pignalberi, Father Quiricus, O.F.M. Conv. *Process.*

Pisarek, Brother Marvellus, O.F.M. Conv. In Ricciardi, p. 340.

Podwapinski, Brother Lawrence, O.F.M. Conv. *Process.*

"Brother Lawrence Remembers." Series of articles appearing in 1964 in *Crusader of Mary Immaculate* magazine, published by the M.I. in Manchester, England.

Poplawski, Brother Pelagius, O.F.M. Conv. *Process.*

Popropek, Stanislaus. *Process.*

Rembisz, Gorgonio. *Process.*

Rosenbaiger, Father Samuel, O.F.M. Conv. *Process.*

Roszkowska, Sophia. *Process.*

Ruszczak, Father Sigismund. "Blessed Maximilian Kolbe at Auschwitz." *Immaculata Reprints Library,* August 1978. Taken from Vatican Radio Broadcast.

Sergius, Brother. *See* Pesiek.

Sieminski, Brother Gabriel, O.F.M. Conv. *Process.* (Also quoted in the *Process* by other Brothers.)
Additional information supplied by Father Giorgio Domanski from Polish sources.

Sienkiewicz, Henry. *Process.*
Vatican Radio Broadcast.

Sobolewski, Joseph. *Process.*

Stemler, Joseph. *Process.*
In Ricciardi, p. 396.

Stella, Father Dominic, O.F.M. Conv. *Process.*

Stryczny, Father Bronislaus, O.F.M. Conv. *Immaculata,* forthcoming.
Testimonies to Cyril Kita and Ferdinandus Kasz, in the *Process* under those names.

Sulatycka, Sister Felicitas. *Process.*

Swies, Brother Ladislaus. *Process.*

Szegidewicz, Jan. Niepokalanow archives: Correspondence with the author dated May 23, 1982, from Brother Ferdinandus Kasz, O.F.M. Conv. Translated by Father Evarist Kleszcz, O.F.M. Conv.
In Dewars.

Szrednicki, Eugene. *Process.*

Sztyk, Brother Felicissimus, O.F.M. Conv. "Misakae No Sono." *Immaculata,* November 1977.

Szweda, Father Conrad. *Process.*

His two-part article on Kolbe in Auschwitz, "Wspomnienia z ostatnich chwil zycia s.p. O. Maksymiliana Marii Kolbe," was published in *The Knight,* Niepokalanow, Poland, in November and December 1945. Translated from the Polish by J. Ligus of Los Angeles.

Vatican Radio Broadcast.

Takashi, Paul Nagai, M.D. *Process.*

Traczyk, John. *Process.*

Umeki, Father Charles. In Sebastiano Botticella's "The Militia of the Immaculata: Fifty Years of Life." Translated by Brother Richard Arnandez, F.S.C. Pages 46–47 and 49.

Unidentified anti-Semitic woman (Rosalia Kobla). *Process.*

Wasowicz, Stanislaus, M.D. *Process.*

Wedrowski, Brother Arnold, O.F.M. Conv. *Process.*

In Mlodozeniec, p. 66.

Wierzba, Brother Jerome, O.F.M. Conv. *Process.*

In Mlodozeniec, pp. 61–62.

Wilk, Stefan P., M.D. Interview by the author, March 1982.

Wlodarski, Francis, M.D. *Process.*

"B1. Maximilian Kolbe at Auschwitz." *Immaculata Reprints Library,* August 1978.

Wojcik, Father Marian, O.F.M. Conv. "Blessed Maximilian Kolbe's Outstanding Venture in Mass Communications." *Immaculata,* August 1972.

Wojtkowski, Thaddeus (Ted). Interview by the author, April 16, 1982, Libertyville, Ill.

Correspondence with the author dated June 11, 1982.

Yamaki, Francis Toshio. *Process.*

Zajac, Mrs. (no first name given). In Mlodozeniec, p. 53.

Zebrowski, Brother Zeno, O.F.M. Conv. *Process.*
In anonymous account attributed to Brother Sergius Pesiek.

ADDITIONAL MATERIALS

Auschwitz 1940–1945: Guide-book Through the Museum.
Krajowa Agencja Wydawnicza.

Domanski, Giorgio, O.F.M. Conv. *I Dati Storici della Vita del P.
Massimiliano M. Kolbe.* Rome: Milizia dell'Immacolata, no
date.

Feig, Konnilyn G. *Hitler's Death Camps: The Sanity of Madness.*
New York and London: Holmes & Meier Publishers, 1981.

Gawalewicz, Adolf. Introduction to Adam Bujak's *Auschwitz-
Birkenau.* Translated from the Polish by Krystyna Bidwell.
Warsaw: Sport i Turystyka, no date.

PERIODICALS

Documentation Catholique 76, no. 1767 (July 1, 1979).

"Father Maximilian M. Kolbe: The Hero of Auschwitz." Special
issue of the *Messenger of St. Anthony.* Padua: St. Anthony's Ba-
silica Conventual Franciscans, October 1971.

Fein, Helen. "Reviewing the Toll: Jewish Dead, Losses and Victims of the Holocaust." In *Shoah,* Spring 1981.

Kemon, George. "Holocaust Priest." In *Our Sunday Visitor,* November 29, 1981.

National Geographic, April 1982 (special supplement).

Various issues of *Immaculata* magazine, 1961 to 1982.

Chronology

January 8, 1894
Raymond Kolbe is born to Julius and Maria (née Dabrowska) Kolbe in Zdunska Wola, Poland.

September 4, 1910
Raymond enters novitiate of Friars Minor Conventual in Lwow, Poland, and is invested with the name Friar Maximilian.

November 22, 1915
At age twenty-one, Maximilian earns a Ph.D. in Philosophy from the Pontifical Gregorian University, Rome.

October 16, 1917
With six confreres, Friar Maximilian founds the Knights of the Immaculata (M.I.).

April 28, 1918
Maximilian is ordained a priest by Cardinal Basilio Pompili in Rome and celebrates his first Mass the next day (April 29) in the Church of Sant'Andrea delle Fratte.

July 1919
Father Maximilian earns Th.D. in Theology from the Franciscans' International College, Rome.

Father Maximilian leaves Rome for Cracow, Poland, where he is assigned to teach church history at the seminary of Friars Minor Conventual. He immediately organizes focus groups of the M.I.

October 1, 1927
Prince John Maria Drucki-Lubecki donates land at Teresin, outside Warsaw, for the beginning of Father Maximilian's City of the Immaculata, known in Polish as Niepokalanow.

February 1930	Father Maximilian leaves Niepokalanow for Nagasaki, Japan, where he establishes Mugenzai no Sono (Garden of the Immaculata). This "city" was largely undamaged in the 1945 atomic bomb explosion over Nagasaki.
1936	Father Maximilian returns to Poland and becomes Guardian at Niepokalanow.
September 19, 1939	Nazis commandeer Niepokalanow and arrest Father Maximilian. He is detained, successively, at Lamsdorf, Amtitz, and Ostrzeszow.
December 10, 1939	Father Maximilian returns to Niepokalanow and reorganizes the friary.
February 17, 1941	Father Maximilian is arrested by the Gestapo and imprisoned in Pawiak Prison, Warsaw.
May 28, 1941	Father Maximilian is transferred to Auschwitz as prisoner number 16,670.
August 1941	As punishment for the escape of one prisoner, SS officer Fritsch chooses ten men from Block 14A to be sent to the starvation bunker. Father Maximilian volunteers to take the place of Sergeant Francis Gajowniczek.
August 14, 1941	Still alive after two weeks in the starvation bunker, Father Maximilian is given a lethal injection.
August 15, 1941	Father Maximilian's body is incinerated at Auschwitz.
October 17, 1971	Father Maximilian is beatified by Pope Paul VI in Saint Peter's Basilica, Rome.
October 10, 1982	Father Maximilian is canonized as a saint by Pope John Paul II.

Author's Note

MANY OF THE recollections of Maximilian Kolbe that make up this book were obtained from personal interviews by myself or others or from written reminiscences, either published or unpublished, many of which have never before appeared in English.

Other witnesses to Kolbe's life and death have shared their memories of him as part of the Beatification Process, a quasi-juridical proceeding of the Catholic Church in which hearings are held to determine the sanctity of an individual. In the principal places that individual lived and worked, those who knew him testify under oath as to his heroic virtues. Each witness answers the same questions, their oral responses being taken down by someone fulfilling the function of court reporter. For the use of the Congregation for the Causes of Saints in Rome, the testimonies—in this case in Polish, Japanese, Italian, and Latin—are rendered in Italian and Latin.

In reporting testimony from the Process, I have often combined answers to more than one question, especially where the respondent refers to the same incident in discussing various characteristics of Kolbe's. Further, since human speech tends to head toward a point, veer off toward something else, and then reverse itself, I have felt no compunction to keep sentences in the order in which they appear. My goal has not been a scholar's literalness but a clear report of what those who knew him thought about Maximilian Kolbe. Faced with a figurative mountain of Process testimonies and dozens of non-Process memoirs of Kolbe, I have had to be selective. In doing so, I have tried to retain as many viewpoints as possible, so that, for instance, I have included a neighbor who knew him well and a Franciscan, rather than two Franciscans. I have also chosen to give longer testimony from, say, twenty people, rather than a paragraph or two from forty. The reader may be sure there has been no effort to edit out, from any source, evidence of the controversy Kolbe sometimes aroused or the opposition he experienced. As much as anyone, I came to this project hoping to find not a plaster saint but a man. That so many witnesses indicate love and admiration for Kolbe is a tribute to the lovableness and magnetism of the subject, not to my editing.

If you have ever looked at a so-called great man and wondered what those who knew him on a day-to-day basis—his housemates, relatives, neighbors, co-workers, bosses, employees, jailers, etc.— thought about him, you have already grasped the thrust of this book, which could just as easily have been called simply "Kolbe by Those Who Knew Him." It differs from those biographies in which a writer uses the known facts of a life, recollections of others, letters, and other writings to compose a portrait that is then interpreted by situating it in a milieu and explaining its significance for that time and place (also a portrait composed and interpreted by the writer). Such biographies can be splendid. Often, however, I have felt that they told me more about the biographer than the subject. I particularly dislike a writer's imagining what the subject *"must* have felt," *"must* have done," where records leave a blank. In the present book—which I prefer to call a documentary rather than a biography—I have tried to stand aside and let those who actually knew him speak. Admittedly, the potential for distortion is present in every witness; still, with so many gazes trained on one man, portraits tend to correct and deepen each other, distortions become evident while the real traits, seen from various perspectives, are highlighted or shadowed in their human complexity as depth is added to the prosaic burghers of Rembrandt by chiaroscuro. For me, Kolbe's moments of anxiety and bursts of wry humor—distortions when seen alone—are the shadows that play across the flat light of his habitual serenity and lifelong seriousness of purpose to produce a portrait recognizable as a real human being.

As for interpreting his significance to human heroism or his place in Polish history, while I have suggested my views, as have some of the witnesses, I have chosen to leave this analysis to the reader. I have done the same with Kolbe's place in the annals of Catholicism, although that, in a sense, is implicit in the Church's having proclaimed him a saint. Certainly the present pope, John Paul II, who considers his countryman a spiritual mentor, would

like to see Kolbe "a patron for our difficult century" and a model "for a world in which hatred and revenge continue to torment human society."

I would like to thank the Order of Friars Minor Conventual, especially Fathers Philip M. Wozniak and Ambrogio Sanna, Postulator of Kolbe's Cause, both of Rome, and the Conventual Franciscans of Marytown, USA, in Libertyville, Illinois, for making 900 pages of Process testimony available for my use.

For help in translating the bulk of this material in just under two weeks from Italian and Latin, I am grateful to Ludovica Longinotti and Brother Richard Arnandez, FSC.

I should also like to thank Brother Raphael Ruffolo, Marytown's Superior, for the community's hospitality; Brothers Martin Schmitz and Camillus Dulude for many special services; Father Bernard Geiger for his advice and generous sharing of sources; Brother Francis Mary Kalvelage for, among other things too numerous to mention, initiating the project, providing me with material and leads on people to interview, actually conducting an interview I couldn't get to, and sharing with me interviews he had done for *Immaculata* magazine; Father Evarist Kleszcz for translations into and out of Polish, especially correspondence with Niepokalanow; and the community for use of portions of materials which have appeared or may in the future appear in *Immaculata,* particularly Brother Felicissimus M. Sztyk's and Father Bronislaw Stryczny's reminiscences of Kolbe, Jan Dudzinski's Auschwitz memories, and Brother Francis Mary's interview with Father Stanley Frejlich.

I am grateful to Brother Juventyn Mlodozeniec of Assisi for his enthusiastic permission to quote from his articles and his book *I Knew Blessed Maximilian,* and to John Haffert and AMI Press for their permission; to *Crusader* magazine, Manchester, England, for excerpts from Brother Lawrence Podwapinski's memoir articles, which appeared in that publication in 1964; to Marytown for permission to quote from Friar Albert Arzilli's and Father Leon Cicchito's recollections of Kolbe in *The Death Camp Proved Him Real,* by Maria Winowska, published in this country by *Prow* Franciscan; to Tom Fox of the *Philadelphia Inquirer* for permission to quote from his interview with Auschwitz survivors, pub-

lished in the *Philadelphia Daily News;* to Brother Ferdinandus Kasz of Niepokalanow for verifying information; to Father John Burdyszek, O.F.M. Conv., and Burns & Oates of London for permission to quote from his book *Father Maximilian Kolbe: Fire Enkindled,* originally published by Clonmore and Reynolds of Dublin; and to the priests and parishioners of Our Lady of the Bright Mount Church, Los Angeles, for translating and verifying information.

My gratitude to the recognized authority on the facts of Kolbe's life and Militia, Father Giorgio Domanski of Rome, for reviewing my manuscript for factual errors; and to Daniel L. Schlafly, Jr., associate professor of history, St. Louis University, and Warren Green of the St. Louis Center for Holocaust Studies, both of whom reviewed background information on Poland and Auschwitz.

I would also like to thank those who personally shared with me their memories of Kolbe: John Dagis, Ted Wojtkowski, Francis Mleczko (and my gratitude to Father James McCurry, O.F.M. Conv., of St. Hyacinth's, Granby, Mass., for permission to quote from his taped interview with Mleczko and for doing a second interview to answer my further questions), Stefan P. Wilk, M.D., Alexsy Kucharski, Sigmund Gorson, and Brother Bartholomew Kalucki.

To my family for "doing it all" so I could do this, my loving thanks and my solemn promise not to have anything to do with saints for at least two weeks.

For many reasons this book is built on prayer as much as research. For prayer support, I should like to thank Alice Williams, Eva Engholm, Judith and Bob Hodgins, Sheila Kalivas, Sister Veronica, O.C.D., Monsignor John V. Sheridan, and all my Franciscan friends.